Sacred
Relationships

Sacred Relationships

A Guide to Authentic Loving

Daniel Raphael

ORIGIN PRESS

Origin Press
1122 Grant Ave., Suite C
Novato, CA 94945
(415) 898-7400

ISBN: 1-57983-001-3

Library of Congress Cataloging-in-Publication Data
Raphael, Daniel, 1943–
    Sacred relationships : a guide to authentic loving / Daniel Raphael.
        p.   cm.
    ISBN 1-57983-001-3 (pbk.)
    1. Spiritual life 2. Interpersonal relations—Religious aspects.
    I. Title.
    BL626.33.R37   98-19126
    291.4′4—dc21   CIP

PRINTED IN THE UNITED STATES OF AMERICA
10 9 8 7 6 5 4 3 2 1

Contents

Contents

Part III: Creating Sacred Relationships

Contents

Values
Skills
Discerning Qualities, Values, and Skills
Self-Caring Is a Skill

The Four "R"s of Basic Education
A Strategy for Intentional Relationship Training
A Developmental Continuum of Relationship
    Skill Training
Why Teach Functional Relationship Skills?

Preface

Most of the problems and issues described in this manual come from an intense period of discovery in my intimate relationship life. Some of the experiences were living nightmares—but instructive ones. I began to probe them consciously and question everything about them. I came to see that relationship issues and spiritual growth in general are connected. It was then that I began to immerse myself in relationship issues to discover their spiritual potential.

During this brief period, so many immediate answers to questions, unusual insights, and serendipitous meetings occurred that I seriously speculated that some sort of spiritual presence was intentionally involved in my life. Because my former wife was a conscious channel for a wise and wonderful being with whom I had numerous conversations, it seemed reasonable to try to contact this unseen helper on my own. I now realize that the discoveries I made during this seminal period formed my basic understanding of the relationship–spirituality connection and also marked the beginning of my conscious and intentional association with celestial beings and angels.

All of these experiences have helped set the stage for this book. For although my fingers did the typing and my heart, mind, and spirit were intimately involved in writing this manual, I was not alone in its creation and development. I eventually learned that a celestial teacher named Ahsha had helped guide the insights of my own relationship experiences and reframe them into living lessons for this manual. He has also become my friend.

It was Ahsha who initially urged me to begin the first draft of *Sacred Relationships*. As the weeks passed, the progress on the book was steady. Eventually Ahsha and I had roughed out the chapters, and the developmental work seemed to come to a close.

Examining the flow of the chapters, I realized that the book seemed to lack closure. I told Ahsha that I suspected the book was not complete and that it seemed to end too abruptly. He responded, "Do not concern yourself with this now." Hoping for a fuller answer, I concentrated on revising the book as much as possible before releasing it to the publisher for editing.

In the coming months many changes came into my life, including considerable emotional pain that I felt deep in my heart regarding my marriage (Alara and I had met in 1993 and were married in 1995). In March of 1997, I seriously thought about filing for divorce, but changed my mind as I thought there may be some spiritual growth yet to be achieved by remaining in the marriage. As the author of a spiritual book about sacred relationships, it seemed the most reasonable thing to do.

By the time Alara returned in July from a long trip out of state, she had come to the same conclusion. She said she thought we had gotten the greatest good out of our marriage and that it was time to move on. I agreed. Though our mutual conclusion was logical, I felt as though I had gone a full round with a heavyweight boxer. No matter how reasonable a conclusion it was, severing the emotional connection between us felt like a knockout blow.

For the next few days I pondered what Alara and I had been through. It was not long before I had one of those profound "Aha!" experiences of insight that answered all my questions. In a flash I had the insight for three new chapters which would provide just the right closure for the book, including the chapter entitled "When the Sacred Relationship Ends."

By November of that year, our divorce was final. The ending of our marriage, a meaningful relationship, was painful yet joyful. It brought to a close an era in my life of immense emotional and spiritual growth and creativity. As I see it, the closure of an intimate relationship does not indicate failure. On the contrary, it means that we have grown enough to exit one relationship and enter another.

Each of my partnerships has presented me with new horizons for growth. Each gave me new ways of experiencing myself in intimate relationship, and of challenging the boundaries of my emotional and spiritual evolution. I also provided my partners with experiences for challenging their own emotional and spiritual limits.

I consider myself fortunate to participate consciously in truly sacred relationships with angels and celestial beings of God's universe of light. These beings never tell me what to believe or how to behave. Instead, they guide me to resources that help me correct my erroneous beliefs and behaviors.

What I have learned from their gentle ways of relating to me helps me in relating to people. Their sacred relationship with me allows me to see my faults and failures in ways that help me overcome them and grow spiritually. In sharing this guidance with you, my hope is that you, too, can experience truly unconditional, fully loving sacred relationships.

Daniel Raphael
Boulder, Colorado
1999

Introduction:
The Challenge of Creating
Sacred Relationships

Sacred Relationships is a developmental guide for personal spiritual growth that prepares the way to create sustainable sacred relationships. Sacred relationship partners treat their relationship as a dynamic setting in which each consciously and intentionally helps the other heal their emotional wounds, which are always pointers to those places where spiritual growth is necessary. The partners lovingly support each other's spiritual growth while they guide each other to emotional wholeness.

Each of us is confronted with relationship difficulties every day. That's why I created this guide, and probably why you picked it up. If you have not already begun to work on your emotional issues, this book may seem demanding. For you who have already begun to work on your emotional issues, this book will show you the way to further healing, and the connection between clearing your emotional issues and spiritual growth.

It is also my hope that you will find this book to be a source of tremendous hope and inspiration for your relationships. It is obvious that relationships between emotionally incomplete and immature persons are settings for much difficulty and tension. The level of our own emotional development can either aid or inhibit the spiritual development of our partner. Knowing this should inspire us to take more responsibility for developing our infinite potential to grow spiritually.

Emotional maturity and spiritual development are the two most important aspects of personal growth. When people work together to create realistic shared goals for themselves as individuals and for the relationship, they begin to explore the endless potential for growth that sacred relationships provide. Very little spiritual development occurs in a formal classroom—such a setting provides intellectual information, though if the student is fortunate, experiential exercises are included. It is our day-to-day life that provides the venue for growing spiritually in every waking hour, wherever we go and whomever we are with. These lessons offer a continuum of interpretation for relationship experiences that enter your own life.

Your life is your classroom for experiential exercises. After you have read this manual, you should be able to more constructively interpret your "homework" in ways that contribute to your emotional healing and spiritual growth. It should remain a good friend and reference for the relationship experiences, problems, and solutions that later come into your life.

Part I
Entering the Spiritual Path

1

Basics of Getting On the Path

The purpose of this chapter is to uncover the basic resources that support your spiritual journey, as well as to point out factors that can inhibit growth. In addition, it provides an orientation to all the lessons that follow. So let us begin!

THE PREMISE: OUR INFINITE SPIRITUAL POTENTIAL

Spirituality is an infinite potential in everyone who has possession of a fully functioning mind, a mind capable of self-consciousness with which spirit can effectively interact to facilitate growth. Spirituality develops most easily when we are of sound mental and emotional state, socially balanced, and morally and ethically attuned. Initially, our spirituality lies dormant, waiting for us to acknowledge its infinite potential.

A KEY QUESTION FOR BEGINNERS

As our spirituality accelerates, our journey leads to progressively more mature levels of spiritual living. Some call it the ascendant journey because the nearly infinite steps involved in spiritual development will eventually bring us into the eternal embrace of our loving Father-Mother Creator.

If you have recently begun your trek as a spiritual traveler, a moment will probably come when the age-old question "What is the purpose of life?" gets converted to "What is the purpose of *my* life?"

The answer seems to have something to do with the maturation that happens as we keep asking the right questions. By working through the many questions that emerge, we experience what I believe is the purpose of life: growing into a sacred and harmonious relationship with God and the universe. To achieve this long-term goal, we must begin by learning how to live in harmonious relationships with other people. In other words, if we are having problems in our relationships with others, we have work to do before we can have a harmonious relationship with God. So we begin on the spiritual path by initiating growth in those areas where we are having the most problems with other people.

BASIC RESOURCES FOR THE SPIRITUAL PATH

Happily, there are numerous resources for those entering the path. These include the static and dynamic environments, consciousness of self, asking questions, free will, living in the present, reflective thinking, wisdom, meditative stillness, and, of course, relationships themselves!

The Static and Dynamic Environment of Growth

The static environment includes the entire physical environment. It is static because, like a mirror, it is nonreactive, providing us with a nonjudgmental view of ourselves as we interact with it. The unresponsiveness of the physical world provides an opportunity for us to learn about ourselves: how and what we think, our beliefs, expectations, opinions, judgments—everything that emanates from our own thinking without the participation of anyone else. Again, the static environment is only a mirror; it is left to us to ask ourselves, "Why did I react as I did?"

The dynamic environment adds the variable of other people, who may react to our behaviors. It is a much more powerful field of influence than the static environment because it is two-sided, and because the interaction can change rapidly.

The physical world is a good place to start to analyze our emotional reactions because after an incident has passed, we have time to ask ourselves questions about our reactions. But relationships do not provide such a luxury. In the dynamic environment of relationships, the other person can, obviously, react to our actions or reactions, which makes the analysis of our emotional reactions far more difficult.

Observing ourselves first in a nonreactive environment makes it much easier to become conscious of how we react to our world without the added complexity of influence by others. Yet, in dynamic environments, when we become aware of ourselves reacting to what others do, we are able to learn even more about ourselves.

Consciousness of Self

Consciousness of self is the fundamental element we need to develop in both environments. Without consciousness, life is a trek through the wilderness of experience without a clue that there may even be a path. With consciousness comes the potential to explore the wilderness of life, discern our options, and choose our unique path of spiritual growth.

Asking Questions

Consciousness is only the first half of the equation of spiritual growth. The other half is the necessity of questioning. Together, these can propel us onto the developmental stages of our spiritual path. They are the initial steps essential for productive, reflective thinking, which we will discuss soon.

Free Will

Will is the commander of decision making. To activate our spiritual growth, we must freely *will* to decide to do so, then *will* to energize our decision. Next, we invite God, or spirit, to help us grow. These steps are prerequisites for initiating our journey on the spiritual path.

Living in the Present

Although we are totally responsible for our life in all its infinite dimensions, there are unlimited resources to support, guide, and counsel us along the path. These are available from our Father-Mother Creator when we simply ask and are open to receive. As our ability to remain in self-awareness increases, our experience of living moves from hour to hour, minute to minute, and finally from moment to moment. We are then living consciously in the moment—aware of ourselves experiencing every moment. It is in the present moment that these unlimited resources truly become available.

Reflective Thinking

Reflective thinking best occurs when we consciously give ourselves a "time out" to be apart from experience. It involves asking questions about our new experience and answering those questions, thus conferring meaning on our lives. We don't need a doctorate in philosophy to gain profound insights, meaning, and wisdom from our experiences by asking questions such as "What is the meaning of this experience for me?" "What am I to learn from this?" "What makes this experience different?"

Experiencing life without asking meaningful questions poses the danger of reducing us to a life that is a series of disconnected attempts to avoid pain and increase pleasure. At its best, reflective thinking provides a time when our conscious mind can sit in a mystical space, holding dialogue with unseen spiritual forces who help us access wise and intuitive insights in answer to our questions.

Wisdom

Wisdom emanates from reflective thinking in the form of insights derived from our experiences. Wisdom can be used to avoid making the same mistake twice, and to duplicate our successes again and again.

Meditative Stillness

Meditative stillness, or silence, is one step beyond reflective thinking. To understand stillness practice, imagine your mind as a small, tranquil pond. When its surface is disturbed, it cannot reflect the sky. But when its waters are still and silent, reflections of otherwise unseen surroundings become visible. Fifteen minutes of stillness each day can yield incredible results. When our mind is in silence, the spirit can "download" great wisdom, insights, and intuitive perspectives without interruption or interference.

Relationships

Relationships provide incredible challenges for growth to those on the spiritual path. Relationships are dynamic opportunities to interact with, influence, and be influenced by others. They provide a skating rink where we are the dancer-skater, choreographer, coach, and audience. If we are perceptive enough, we can observe ourselves as mortals-becoming-spirit, as spiritual infants striving to grow up.

FACTORS THAT CAN INHIBIT GROWTH

There are at least two key factors that can inhibit the fulfillment of our spiritual potential.

Failure to Make Decisions

To grow spiritually we must decide to become self-aware, decide to discern the possible paths of our growth, consciously choose from among those options, decide to take action to implement our choices, and decide to reflect on and give meaning to our experiences. Without such constant decision making, we have put our spiritual development on hold.

An Unbalanced Ego

Persons with an unbalanced ego perceive themselves as having greater or lesser value than other people. In simple terms, our ego can exist in one of three states. In the balanced state, the ego perceives itself in balanced relationship to other people. In the first type of unbalanced ego state, the ego is out of balance as evidenced by a poor self-image and a lack of self-esteem and self-confidence; this makes us ineffectual as individuals and as partners. With the second type of unbalanced ego, the imbalance shows up as narcissism, arrogance, conceit, and selfishness. These two states of an inadequate ego cause separation from other people and a discrepancy between who we think we are and who we really are.

As you read this book, bear in mind this essential list of the rich resources we carry with us, as well as the factors that can hold us back. Obstacles will surely appear along the path. They can serve to stimulate more growth if we engage them with our will—the subject of our next lesson.

2

Will:
The Forgotten Well
of Personal Power

Will is as important to the spiritual path as love and forgiveness, for without the use of will, neither love nor forgiveness is even possible. We must *will* to love and we must *will* to forgive in order to grow spiritually. We must *will* to energize our relationships to create greater personal happiness and social satisfaction. Without the conscious use of our will to overcome everyday difficulties, the growth of our soul is hampered and restricted.

THE "I AM" SOURCE OF THE POWER OF WILL

All God-centered religions teach that human beings are created in the image of God. This means that in some mysterious way, we as individuals have within us an aspect of God that empowers us just as God is empowered. That aspect is *will*. From the divine point of view, will is synonymous with the concept of I AM. We will return to this important theme throughout this book.

When Moses went up on Mount Horeb, he asked God for God's name so he could share it with the Israelites. As we read in the Book of Genesis, God replied, "I AM that I AM." But who or what is this I AM? Many theologies contain logical discussions of who and what God is, revealing truths about God in a linear, verbal form. It may also be effective to dialogue directly with God so we can understand intuitively how the I AM source of power—our free will—exists and operates in each of us.

THE CENTRAL ROLE OF WILL

To understand the role of will, consider its place in relation to the other parts of our being:

The brain is a complex physical-electrical organ. It is much like a computer, with metaphorical circuit boards, microchips, wires, and storage devices.

Mind is like the software of a computer. Our brain comes with "mind software" already installed. Fortunately, the software can be rewritten.

Personality, in very simple terms, is the unique totality of our being that distinguishes us from one another.

Ego, also in very simple terms, is our perceived self in relationship to others.

Will is the captain, the decision maker and overseer of our mind, so powerful it can even decide to rewrite the software programs of the mind.

God-within is the I AM Presence, the fragment of God resident in our very person. Much like a pilot who guides a ship into harbor, God-within can help guide our decisions, if we *will* to accept its advice.

I Am is an individuation of the I AM FATHER-MOTHER GOD in this life expression, whose sacred task is to grow spiritually and eventually return to the Source, the I AM, in Paradise.

THE FOUR POSITIONS OF WILL

1. Will-less

We can be will-less by failing to make decisions or by not being willing to take action to fulfill the decisions we make. These two situations are common, and they cause many of life's problems. They are learned behaviors that often reflect inadequate childhood role models.

Some of us were raised not to make decisions but to be compliant, obedient, and pleasing and deferring to others. Many people even seek psychic and spiritual guidance to avoid decision-making responsibilities. That is, they ask for counsel but fail to make decisions that shape their life based on the input they receive. The good news is: Regardless of your upbringing, you can change how you use your will to make decisions.

2. Willful

Webster's dictionary defines *willful* as both "obstinately and often perversely self-willed" and "done intentionally; deliberate." By *willful* I am referring here to the use of will that is biased and ego-based. Biased decision making bends the outcome to our benefit, ahead of consideration for others. An ego that is out of balance in its perceived value of itself in relationship to others tends to make self-centered decisions. This results in a "me first" or a "you first" outcome, when the best outcome would be "us together."

3. In Harmony with God's Will

This position is what I call actively and powerfully passive. That is, we wait for the will of God to become evident in our lives, then we act.

It is least powerful when believers rest upon God's will so passively that they become will-less. I have known many sincere religious people who lay down their will to God but *fail* to integrate their will with God's. They placidly wait for God to act in their lives—and are still waiting. Or they fail to discern when God does act in their lives and do not take the necessary follow-on action. In either case, they place their lives on hold.

4. Co-Creative Will

This is the most powerful combination of an active and passive expression of will. To use will co-creatively, we must listen, be observant, and stay alert to become aware of God's will in our lives. The process begins by asking God to fulfill a request (e.g., "Father, please grant this or something better according to Your will for my and others' highest and greatest good"). Then wait, observe, and trust that God will provide right and perfect answers to our prayer requests. Even if they are not fulfilled, remember, God's will has still been done!

But even before we make requests of God, we must believe, have faith, and trust that God will truly act in our lives; then we can ask for His direction co-creatively. Once we have asked for direction, we must "wait upon the Lord" while we observe the flow of events to see how God is responding. At this point we will observe that a variety of options become available, requiring that we must decide which option seems most in alignment with God's will for our life. Next, we will need to muster our courage to act powerfully, making a co-creative demand upon the resources of the universe for the fulfillment of what we have chosen (decided) to fulfill with God as our partner.

Here is an example I use: "Dear God and angels, with your participation I *will* to co-create _____ for the highest and greatest good of all concerned, according to Your will for this situation." As you can see, this is an invitation to co-create. If the invitation is not accepted, no harm is done, for neither God nor His angels will participate. If they do participate, then we have God and His angels to help bring into manifestation what is called forth into creation by us. If they participate, we know that it will be in divine order, for the highest and greatest good of all concerned. Further, by doing this we do not wait for good things to come to us, but actively call them into existence with God's help. We are saying, "Hey, universe! I'm ready for this. Let's go for it!"

Having done all this, it is time to observe the results of our request, trusting that the outcome will be in alignment with God's plan. Often people get confused at this point, when they see that what they have co-creatively requested to come into existence does not come into being. This is when *more trust* is needed in order to accept that the command was or will be fulfilled, but not as we had expected.

Here, then, is a short course for acting co-creatively with God:

• Believe.
• Have faith.

- Trust.
- Ask.
- Decide.
- Wait and observe.
- Gather courage to act.
- Trust some more!

UNIVERSAL RULES FOR THE EXPRESSION OF WILL

Being "created in God's image" has a special significance. Because every thought of God is a perfect expression of *will*, there is no time lapse between the will of God and its manifestation; what God wills, *is*. Being created in God's image, we have the power to will to co-creatively participate in God's all-powerful will. Being conscious of *having will* places us in the highest position of personal, ethical, moral, and spiritual responsibility. As beings indwelled by God we need to be aware of three simple universal principles concerning the use of will.

1. The Inviolability of Self-Will

Self-will is an inviolable aspect of God's free-will creatures. God has not, does not, and will not interfere with the exercise of self-will. God does not accept responsibility for our actions. We act and we are responsible for those actions.

2. Responsibility for Will

There is a special reason for the gift of self-will. Without the potential for total freedom and total responsibility for self-willed decisions, the potential for complete, fulfilling spiritual growth in the infinity of time would be denied to us. God limits Himself to provide us with the possibility of perfecting our spirit-potential on our own terms. To become like God, we must follow the biblical command of Jesus: "Be ye perfect, as your Father in Heaven." The purpose of self-will is to become perfect, no matter how long that takes. We continue this journey to perfection even in the afterlife.

3. Responsibility to Will

Just as we are responsible for the use of our will, we are responsible to use our will. This is so because if we do not *will*, we simply do not grow spiritually. The potential for growth cannot be fulfilled until we make choices, invoke our will, and take action. We are responsible *to* will as well as responsible *for* will; we are as responsible for our *omission* to will as we are for our *commission* to will.

Here's an example of omission of will: Suppose you are the only bystander at the scene of an automobile accident, and you have been trained in CPR. The victim, having been thrown from her car, is lying on the street, unconscious. Her tongue is relaxed in her throat, blocking her windpipe. You can see that she is not breathing. You decide to do nothing, and the victim dies due to suffocation. Are you responsible for her death because of your failure to act?

Though you did not willfully cause the victim's death, you did not prevent it either. The point is that whether we think we live one life, pass "Go," and proceed directly to heaven, or whether we believe we live many lives, we can be assured that we won't be let off the hook by *not* making choices. Wrong decisions and actions are always possible, but these are mitigated by sincere intent and best choice of action. No one, not even God, can ask you to do better than your very best. Our sincere intent and best action are all that is asked for.

Once we become conscious of God's influence in our life, we can accelerate our spiritual, mental, emotional, social, and personal progress faster than ever by willing to do God's will. As soon as we take this proactive stance in our spiritual life, we begin the conscious journey to become more fully Godlike, more perfect, and more perfectly loving in all of our relationships.

3

Evolving Our Consciousness: Achieving the "I AM" State

Three states of existence unfold in the course of our spiritual evolution: *doing, being,* and *I AM.* Moving through these stages of our spiritual evolution is much like being athletes in training. The early stages are tough, but the accomplishments are visible. Later stages require more concentration, but the rewards are tremendous.

States of Existence and Consciousness and Centers of Activity

Existence	Consciousness	Center of Activity
doing	external	material world
being	external/internal	discovery
I AM	internal/universal	expression

This table lists levels of existence, states of consciousness, and related centers of activity. It provides a conceptual "sieve" to sort out the type of *intentional life* we want to live. It can help us make hundreds of small intentional decisions that move us to the next higher state of existence.

The ideal is to consciously move from the "doing" state, through the "being" state, to the "I AM" state, experiencing along the way everything each state has to teach us. This process may take a lifetime or may be brief, depending on the earnestness of our efforts to grow.

THE "DOING" STATE

In this state of existence, a person is fully identified with what he does in the external world. At a party among strangers it is easy to pick out such people by listening to their "I" statements: "Hi, my name is Charles Paulson. I'm the high school football coach."

"Doing-people" derive their self-worth and self-image from the outer world, where their state of consciousness is really based. Their activities are centered around materialistic pursuits. Material goods are evidence of achievement and validation of their success. Achieving external goals gives their life meaning and value.

Most of us have been brought up to be "doing-people," to think of ourselves as being what we do. The "doing" state has been characteristic of Western culture, particularly since the early phases of the Industrial Revolution. During this phase of our culture, people became a more integral part of the processes of production in order to earn a living.

When Europeans first immigrated to the United States, they brought their "doing-identities" with them. Open any phone book in America and the evidence of this is everywhere in names such as Sawyer, Cartwright, Miller, Weaver, Carpenter, Smith, Wright, Brewer, Master, Chandler, and Cooper. These days, many Americans have become so identified with their work that they have unfortunately become like marketplace commodities, rather than spiritual beings who happen to be earning a living.

"Doing-people" can be found in all walks of life. But this lifestyle is fast becoming obsolete. Those in managerial and corporate executive positions who have "doing" as their focus are particularly vulnerable to extinction because the business of running a corporation has changed dramatically. Corporations have had to become flexible organizations driven by technological and marketing discoveries rather than by hierarchies of authority. Managers and executives in globally competitive corporations must not only *do* managerial and executive tasks but *be* managerial and executive in their consciousness. This is an example of the natural evolution of states of consciousness from "doing" to "being."

THE "BEING" STATE

Moving to the "being" state of existence is the next step. In this state, a person has fulfilled much of her drive for "doing" and perhaps wonders, "Now what?" At this point life becomes really interesting, for the center of activity of the "being" state is discovery. Discovery provides an expanding sense of wonder and awe about ourselves.

A big shift in American culture occurred in the 1960s and 1970s when people began "dropping out" of mainstream activities to pursue lives of discovery. They no longer identified themselves with what their parents did for a living. They began to explore new career and lifestyle options. The question then became not "What do you do?" but "Hey, *how* are ya doin'?" Hipsters of those days might have responded, "Mellow, real mellow."

The prevailing state of consciousness evolved from "doing" to "feeling" or "being," from the external to the internal. People began to seek activities that supported the way they wanted to feel all the time. This period was the first hint that the "being" state was becoming culturally acceptable.

THE "I AM" STATE

The "I AM" state of existence is the next step after the "being" state, but there is no sudden or clear demarcation between the two. As we continue our journey of self-discovery, we naturally begin to express our inherent I AM identity.

What is the I AM state of existence? It is the sure knowledge and full acceptance that I AM is the *mortal expression* of the eternal I AM THAT I

AM, which resides as a fragment of Itself in the very core of each of us. As we live more of our life in the I AM state, our center of activity becomes the expression of this Godhood. Our consciousness has now become "internal/universal." We recognize the divinity within us, and express that center of activity in all of our relationships.

The I AM state of consciousness is a state of spiritual mastery. The master student has achieved the full, living expression of the God-within. In this state of spiritual existence, a person is more than *being* loving, joyful, and peaceful, she has *become* the living expression and embodiment of love, joy, and peace. In this state of consciousness, the person *is* love, peace, joy, contentment, satisfaction, and the full, living, co-creative partner of the Creator-God Consciousness within.

In this state of spiritual consciousness, a person can authentically say, "I am love, I am peace, I am God-becoming, I am wisdom, I am charity, I am patience," and so on. He is not just being peaceful or being loving, but has become a living *definition* of love, peace, joy, happiness, and contentment. He exhibits, lives, thinks, and *is* the I AM expression of that state.

4

Problems:
A Source of Soul Growth

Why is the journey on the spiritual path so difficult? Why do so many problems get in our way? Why do so many daily hassles distract our attention from our spiritual practices? What is the source of the endless series of problems that come into our life?

Solving problems allows us to break down the boulders blocking our spiritual path into gravel that will support our journey. In the short run, doing this is more difficult than simply avoiding our problems. Yet in the long run, confronting our problems as they arise makes our spiritual journey far more manageable.

Consciousness is needed in order to accept and then derive lessons from our problems. When difficult problems arrive—and they always will—the conscious spiritual student eagerly asks, "What am I to learn from this?"

OVERCOMING NEGATIVE PROGRAMMING

Probing our problems is a delicate inquiry because the process leads to intimately personal and often painful places. Our search will pull us deep within ourselves, and perhaps into places usually considered "out of bounds." So let us start by beginning before the beginning.

According to metaphysical tradition, our beginning was in eternity, with God as the source of our soul. When we were created, we immediately became separate souls emanating from the mother-soul of God, waiting for a material body, brain, and mind to use for the further development of this soul. We were pure, without flaw, without sin. This state of perfect purity continued into our early childhood.

Unfortunately, from the time of conception until the time that we began making our own decisions, we were subjected to intensive parental indoctrination. During those early years, we were a blank slate of innocence being programmed for the rest of our life. As we grew, parental authority continued to reinforce that indoctrination, and even now, most of us continue to live according to our parents' admonitions.

For those of us who have consciously and intentionally chosen the spiritual path, our early programming all too often puts us in conflict with others and, worse, with who we really are. We have the rest of our lives to resolve this indoctrination, hopefully freeing ourselves to uncover the soul perfection we had as an original emanation from God. The number and difficulty of personal problems that souls being born today must overcome is enormous, considering that a majority of families in our culture are dysfunctional. Yet these very problems provide a fertile field for producing tremendous soul growth.

THE PURPOSE OF PROBLEMS

The purpose of problems is for us to grow spiritually from the experience of overcoming them, by learning to make decisions that contribute to the growth of our soul. While I believe that angels are created as (almost) perfect beings, we are designed to achieve perfection developmentally. We do this through our experiences as ordinary human beings in a material world. The metaphysical tradition indicates that we agreed to this process at the time of the birth of our soul. We did this because although God knows all, is all, and is everywhere present, God lacks access to the specific experiences that each of His created children will live through, until we actually have these experiences!

The experience of overcoming problems in order to grow spiritually is our gift to God so He can come to know His universe more fully. It is our personal way of helping God become more than solely the Creator! Our most advanced approach to doing this is to will to do God's will in all aspects of our life. Our gift to ourselves, the universe, and God is to experience all the combinations of experience that we meet—successfully. That means working through and solving a vast array of problems.

Think of it in terms of this metaphor: Problems that require difficult moral and ethical decisions provide us with the opportunity to add "weight" to our soul. At first, we come into this world with a feather-light soul. Growing our souls in weight and substance is necessary if our soul is to survive death. Many problems we are confronted with, particularly those involving the welfare of other people, provide us with the opportunity to consciously add weight to our soul. Even small ethical decisions made correctly add to its substance. The "weight" of our soul increases rapidly when we *consciously* embrace our problems.

INTERPRETATIONS AND BELIEFS ABOUT PROBLEMS

When does a difficult situation become a problem? The only difference between the two is the beliefs we have about any given difficulty. These beliefs determine our interpretations of the situation. Situations especially become problems for personal growth when we respond with negative emotions. *It is our emotional reaction and our verbal and physical responses that identify whether a situation becomes a problem—and therefore an opportunity for personal growth.* Ultimately, the problem is not what is going on outside us, but what is going on inside our mind—our interpretation of the situation and our reaction to it.

Here's a simple example: You get ready to go to work, go to your car, and find that it has a flat tire. How do you react? What words do you express, aloud or in your mind?

Version 1, using self-talk: "Hmm, looks like I will probably be a little late, but it will only take ten minutes to change the tire."

Version 2, shouting at the top of your lungs: "The blasted tire is flat! The world's against me! I'll never get to work on time!"

Same flat tire, same situation to deal with—what's the difference?

Again, the difference between problems and difficult situations is how we interpret the situation. Ultimately, our interpretations of situations and events around us derive from the beliefs we were taught as children.

In Version 1, the person sees the problem as part of the continuum of existence—just one more event in the stream of experience coming into his life to encounter, interpret, adjust to, and work through. This person perceives his life as integrated with the universe and all its processes. Difficult events are simply seen as situations that need to be worked through more thoughtfully.

In Version 2, the person's interpretation transforms the situation into a problem. He sees the situation as separate from himself, outside of himself. This person sees his whole world in terms of separation: His world must be conquered and subdued for him to have balance and happiness.

The interpretation given to any situation reflects the observer's beliefs about his relationship to the world outside of himself. As Dr. Wayne Dyer has taught, when we change our beliefs we change what we see. That is, believing is seeing.

Whether people see a situation as a problem or simply another ordinary event in their day is readily apparent from how they talk about it.

When a passerby sees a flat tire on your car and notices you dressed for work and pulling the jack out of the trunk, he might say, "Looks like you've got a real problem there." Your response could be, "No, not really. I just have a flat tire."

PROBLEMS WITH OTHER PEOPLE

As spiritual students on a spiritual path on a material planet with other fallible human beings, we really have no "problems with other people." That may seem like an odd statement, but from the loving, universal perspective of Master Consciousness, *all* of our interactions with other people provide settings for our spiritual unfoldment. Any given interaction reflects the stage of our spiritual development and maturity.

Even when a problem is directly caused by another person, how we respond to that situation is completely our decision and, once made, is our responsibility.

In summation: How we react emotionally and respond to a situation defines whether we have a problem or not. Further, our decision to react to another person who is having a problem determines whether we become part of their problem.

THE PROBLEM WITH OURSELVES

The situation "out there" is never the real problem—the problem is our response. "The problem with ourselves" is that we all too often encounter situations to which we respond in knee-jerk fashion, instantaneously taking action without thinking of the consequences, which then makes us miserable.

The insidious aspect of this process is that regardless of how it may appear, we always make some form of decision in every situation. But we have erroneously come to believe that once a situation occurs, there is no gap between observing and reacting—the two are instantaneously locked together. In fact, our mind does take time, even if it is only a millionth of a second, to make a decision about the situation before responding. The sequence goes like this:

Whether we are conscious of it or not, when a situation arises, it is always followed by our:

- Perception.
- Analysis of the situation.
- Deliberation: Problem or no problem?
- Decision: Problem!
- Emotional response/reaction.

Sometimes people move into an active response even before their body has had time to develop the symptoms of emotional reaction such as clenched fists, red face, rapid pulse and respiration, or heightened blood pressure. For example, a fellow hears a dog yelping outside of his house. He loves animals, so the yelping causes him concern. He jumps up from his chair, opens the door, and sees his neighbor kicking a dog. The fellow runs down the steps, charges the man, and punches him in the face. He continues to hit and kick the man until other neighbors subdue him. Soon a police cruiser pulls up to the curb, where a crowd of folks has gathered. The police officer asks, "Why did you assault this guy? You could be in a lot of trouble if you don't have a good reason."

Response: "I didn't have a choice. He was hurting the dog. I just saw him kicking his dog and I punched him out. I wasn't thinking and I got really angry. What he was doing really upset me. Hey, it ain't my problem. Okay?"

Some folks standing around would probably say, "Yeah, he didn't have a choice; the guy was going to kill his dog if he didn't get stopped." Like the guy who assaulted the dog owner, they observe, then react.

Whether our "problems" are instant interpretations of situations, as in this example, or of situations that develop slowly as we become dissatisfied with the way we are living, we make real decisions about how we respond and how we react emotionally. Until we become aware that it is our decisions that determine whether we have problems, we will often continue to rationalize, justify, blame, and refuse to take responsibility for the outcomes, no matter how much it hurts us or others. And until we accept responsibility for the decisions we make in the millionth of a second before reacting and responding, we will be unable to even see that we have a problem with ourselves—like the impetuous neighbor who said, "Hey, it ain't my problem. Okay?"

OVERCOMING THE PROBLEM WITH OURSELVES

Only when we consciously understand that the pain and unhappiness we experience is directly connected to our own decisions can we begin to make different decisions.

To do so, we must have:

1. Conscious dissatisfaction with the way we are living.
2. A conscious awareness that our dissatisfaction is caused by the decisions we make. Through working in prisons for more than ten years, I discovered that although many inmates were dissatisfied with the way they were living, and they told me so repeatedly, most of them were unable to acknowledge, let alone accept, that their unhappiness was directly connected to the decisions they had made in the past.
3. A consciously free and complete admission and acceptance of responsibility for the decisions we make and the unhappiness we feel.
4. To overcome the "problem with myself," I must not only have the consciousness developed in the steps above, I must *will* to take action to change how I decide, react, and respond to difficult situations. My recovery and healing can only begin when I *will* to do so. Except in the case of mental illness, the solutions to problems with ourselves and problems with other people lie in the province of our own consciousness and will.

THE ROOT OF OUR PROBLEMS: UNRESOLVED EMOTIONAL ISSUES

Why do we react negatively to some situations and call them problems and not others? Why do we have problems with ourselves and with others? What is the source that causes us to react negatively in the first place?

The source is our unresolved emotional issues. Let me give you an example:

During lunchtime in a large tire store, two young male employees are chatting with each other at their desks while eating sandwiches. One is stretched out in his chair with his feet on his desk and his lunch in his lap. An older male supervisor walks into the area to help a customer and in passing says, "Yo, Jimmy, it'd look better to the public and for our company image if you'd keep your feet off your desk. Thanks."

Jimmy slowly draws up his legs, puts his feet on the floor, stands up, and, with his face strawberry red, wads up his sandwich wrapper and slam-dunks it into the wastebasket next to his desk. He motions to his fellow employee and they walk rapidly into the warehouse. Once past the door Jimmy says, "That arrogant turkey is just like my father—always concerned about what other people think of what I'm doing. God, that hacks me off!"

His friend responds, "Hey, Jimmy, what's your problem? He didn't jump down your throat about having your feet on the desk. Relax, will ya?"

Why did Jimmy react and respond as he did? Almost certainly he reacted because he interpreted the situation through the filter of unresolved issues regarding his father and perhaps other males who were in parental authority roles when he was a child.

WHAT IS AN EMOTIONAL ISSUE?

What is a hang-up? What is an issue? An issue is the residue from any past unresolved experience that contains negative emotional energy. Some people call the accumulation of our emotional issues personal baggage.

When the supervisor came into the office area and asked Jimmy to move his feet, in a millionth of a second—without his knowing it—Jimmy's mind raced back to several incidents when his father had severely chastised him in front of other people for behavior his father thought would displease others. Jimmy felt, both as a child and upon mulling it over thousands of times in the years since, that his father was more concerned about what other people thought than about his son's feelings. His dad was more interested in punishing him than in using the incident to explain and teach him what was inappropriate about his behavior.

When the supervisor made his request, all Jimmy saw was his father's unrelenting tirade, unjustified victimization, and his own worthlessness.

What are Jimmy's issues? Father figures, authority figures, older males perhaps, victimization, rejection, deep feelings of worthlessness, lack of feeling appreciated, and probably many more.

Here's another example, but I'll leave it open-ended for you to analyze. Betty was a woman in her thirties, very attractive and well educated, who enjoyed outdoor sports and cultural activities and had many admirers. She dated often, and several times over the years had dated only one man at a time, sometimes for many months. Betty had been engaged a few times but had never been married, and she was concerned that she might never find the right guy.

Upon questioning, Betty freely discussed her intimate relationships and no issues or hang-ups emerged immediately to indicate what was causing the problem. As our discussion continued and we worked through each intimate relationship, a pattern began to reveal itself. Betty had been selecting potential mates whom she slowly discovered to be manipulative, domineering, and unfaithful, and the discoveries usually came fully to light only after she became engaged or shortly before the wedding.

What issues would cause Betty to choose potential mates such as these? Why wasn't she learning from her pattern? And what do you think caused her to have these issues in the first place?

Problems with other people can help us grow spiritually only when we live consciously enough in the moment to ask questions such as "Why is this situation in my face right now?" or "What do I have to learn from this situation?" Put another way: "What is this situation trying to tell me?" "What issue am I supposed to be working on now?"

Betty's emotional reactions and her negative spoken and unspoken verbal responses to relationship situations are her clues to her unresolved emotional issues. Even when problems are blatantly caused by the other person, when we react with negative emotions (whether aloud or silently), we still need to discover and work on our related issues.

The following is a line of questioning that relates to the standard of spiritually developed Master Teachers. (Examples of Master Teachers include Jesus, Buddha, Paramahansa Yogananda, Krishnamurti, and the Dalai Lama.) Ask questions like these to help you discover what your issues are: "How would the Master *feel* in this situation? How would the Master *react to* this situation? What would the Master *do* in this situation?"

As discussed earlier, most of our personal issues arise as a result of faulty prenatal, infant, childhood, and pre-adult training and programming. There was either (1) an absence of appropriate training and socialization; (2) training or socialization that was inappropriate or in error; (3) the presence of individuals who modeled inappropriate, incorrect, immoral, unethical, or illegal behaviors, or caused physical, verbal, sexual, or emotional abuse or neglect; (4) a combination of these.

Our early learning experiences and socialization provide a filter through which all our adult experiences are interpreted. When there is a match between an unresolved negative emotional situation from childhood and a similar occurrence today that reminds us of the earlier one, we will almost always have a negative emotional reaction similar to the one we had as a child. Such a match, combined with our negative emotional reaction, is evidence that negatively charged energy surrounds that prior childhood memory. That memory and the negatively charged emotions surrounding it create an emotional issue.

NO SHORTCUTS!

There are no shortcuts to spiritual bliss. We cannot achieve spiritual nir-
vana by avoiding our issues. We can give away all our material wealth,
enter a monastery, and be of humble service to others for the rest of our
life, but in doing that we avoid making those tough day-to-day decisions
about how to live that add weight to our souls.

This lesson has taken us from far outside of ourselves to deep within.
We have examined problems ranging from a flat tire to the origins of our
rage. While we might rail against God about the unfair world we live in, the
bigotry we experience, and the inequity of our material lives, our beliefs
provide us with an agenda of lessons to be worked through during our lifetime. Without problems, without difficult situations, without tension in our
lives, we would have no desire to grow and develop. Only when we consciously grasp the hammer of our will and strike it against the anvil of our
issues can we forge the spiritual growth and happiness we yearn for.

Part II
Healing the Heart

5

Living Consciously
in the Moment

The concept of living consciously in the moment is one of the bedrock principles of intentional, spiritual living. *Being conscious in the moment means being continuously aware of ourselves experiencing ourselves.* It means being intimately aware of our internal reactions, feelings, and thoughts about what is occurring. This awareness is integral to the intentional use of will, love, and forgiveness.

MINDING THE PRESENT

Living consciously in the moment uses the information contained in each moment to make decisions about the next moment. We have to relax and slow down in order to do this, so that each decision is made with care, our thoughts are carefully developed, our words chosen and spoken carefully. Until we have developed this facility of "mindful" living, it is difficult to live consciously in the moment when we have a complex lifestyle.

Living consciously in the moment also provides the only means to see the tangible link between our beliefs, negative emotional responses that need to be healed, and the actions we take. The reactions of our body (rapid pulse, shallow breathing, sweaty palms, tensed muscles, and so on) and the emotions we are feeling (fear, anger, resentment, hostility, envy, for example) arise from our subconscious mind. These negative bodily responses and emotions come from beliefs the mind created from memories of similar situations in our past. Whatever may be occurring in the present moment, our subconscious mind operates only according to the logic of past situations. *It is reacting not to what is actually happening now but to what it believes is occurring, based on interpretations of and beliefs about prior experiences.*

In less than a second, our subconscious mind races through hundreds of remembered scenarios, bringing up scenes filled with emotionally charged words, interpretations, and beliefs. It is looking for similar situations from the past so it can prepare the body to react to the present situation in a similar way. That is why, when we watch action and adventure movies, our emotions are stirred up and our bodies react by releasing adrenaline. The subconscious mind believes the movie is a true "fight or flight" situation. Whether we feel the passion of rage or of lust, our subconscious mind has leapt ahead of reality to form erroneous conclusions about the present situation, based on beliefs from past situations. It doesn't know the difference between a real-life experience, the memory of a real-life experience, or a vicarious experience from a movie or television program. The scenes that flow from our subconscious mind's "video library" mix with the words of the actors and our own interpretations and beliefs about what we are seeing on the screen as it relates to our past.

Our erroneous interpretations are based on beliefs we either developed by ourselves or received from someone in authority. The interpretations are often painful, usually inaccurate, and can cause problems that then need to be healed.

HEALING THROUGH SELF-OBSERVATION

Healing cannot begin until the conscious mind, using reasoning, steps in and says, "Whoa! Time out! This is just a movie, not reality. This movie only looks like a similar situation and episode that happened in your life several years ago."

The best thing that we can do *in the moment* when we become aware that our body and emotional reactions do not fit the present situation is to excuse ourselves and retreat to where we can review what occurred. The conversation we have with ourselves in those moments might go like this: "Okay, my body tensed up. Emotionally I feel (embarrassed/angry/resentful/spiteful). What was going through my mind to make me feel that way? It was just my co-worker talking too loudly. Why did my body and emotions react as they did? What situation did this incident remind me of?"

At that point, review those shadowy memory pictures to help determine what your mind was telling you. Not many people can be objective about their own emotional states, so ask a friend to help you analyze what occurred in your thinking and what interpretations and beliefs you were operating on.

When asking a friend to help, what we don't need is someone to give us justifications and rationalizations for how we reacted. On the other hand, some emotional reactions are fully justified. Learning the difference is an important part of the healing process, and it takes a mature, experienced, and balanced person to do that kind of discernment.

When we live consciously in the moment, each day becomes an opportunity to improve our discernment and work on our healing. Each encounter in every relationship gives us a chance to observe ourselves. Bosses, intimate and distant relatives, friends, and antagonists all provide the screen on which to observe ourselves. We can begin in the morning, as we prepare to go to work or school, and continue as we interact with co-workers, teachers, or other students. We can observe ourselves closely on our commute, as we enter our living space, as we prepare meals, bathe, play, talk on the telephone, prepare to retire for the night, and so on. In a certain sense we must become psychological and emotional anthropologists with only one subject to observe: ourselves. *Remember, it is not what is outside of ourselves that makes us react emotionally, it is our interpretation of what is occurring, guided by our beliefs about similar past experiences.*

Unless we carefully observe ourselves, we become so enmeshed with the world of events and situations that we do not learn from them easily or quickly. Then, learning occurs only after repeated exposures to the same or similar painful and difficult situations and events, much like the dilemma of the main character in the movie *Groundhog Day*. Until we become consciously aware of ourselves and stop reacting inappropriately, we are as much a part of the problem as the difficulties of the situation itself.

LINKING OUR EMOTIONS WITH MEMORIES

Each day will contain many opportunities for growth through situations that remind us of every painful childhood situation we need to work through. As long as we live consciously in each moment, we will be aware of our first reactions as they occur in our body. This is the most important moment of recovery and healing. Our heart pounding, shallow breaths, sweaty hands, and tight muscles in our fists, neck, jaw, and belly are all signs that our mind has already interpreted the immediate situation as a threat. Most often there will be no actual or immediate threat. As soon as we recognize bodily symptoms, we should almost simultaneously become aware of the shift in our emotional state. The next question to ask is, "What emotions am I aware of?"

Healing practitioners, therapists, or doctors can help us consciously review the continuum of our childhood memories to find those that are painful and hold negative emotional energy. Then they can help us process the memory of those situations to release the energy in them, extract the wisdom from them, and replace erroneous beliefs with healthy ones.

Even without a therapist or healing practitioner, however, we can live moment to moment and observe how our body reacts and how our emotional state changes as we enter into new situations and relationships. We can listen to what we say to and about ourselves inside our mind. When we do this, life becomes a practice of meditation in action—a spiritual way of life that can be more demanding than life as practiced by contemplative religious orders living quietly in remote monasteries.

WORKING IT THROUGH

Let's expand the story about Jimmy in the tire store, presented in the previous chapter, to show how this process works.

After his friend responds, "Hey, Jimmy, what's your problem? He didn't jump down your throat about having your feet on the desk. Relax, will ya?" Jimmy is a lot cooler. He responds, "You're right. Thanks for telling me to relax. Would you do me a favor? Help me work through this. I don't want to react like that anymore."

In the warehouse, Jimmy begins to review each part of his reaction to Jack.

"My therapist told me that when I get into a situation like this, I should live in the moment and feel what is going on in my body, the emotions I am having and the thoughts I'm thinking. I gotta report this to him. I think this situation is really important; it seems connected to something that happened when I was a kid."

Eddie asks, "Well, how *did* your body react?"

"I was okay when I started eating my lunch. Until Jack stopped and turned to face me, I was relaxed. As soon as I saw him towering above me, my whole body tensed up—my belly muscles tensed up really hard. At the same time, the muscles in my shoulders, neck, and arms got so rigid I couldn't even move.

"When he walked away, I felt a red-hot rage start to spread all over my face, then down my neck and back and into my arms and legs. Then I stood up. It was a good thing that Jack didn't come back over to me, 'cause I would've punched his lights out. God, I was angry.

"It's hard to pin down my thoughts. I wasn't thinking too clearly then, but I do remember the pictures that flashed through my mind. My therapist said to remember the pictures because they are more closely linked to past emotional experiences than words are. The first picture that flashed into my mind was of when I was about three or four years old. Then I saw pictures of similar experiences that occurred all through my childhood until I was bigger than my dad. He never bothered me much after that 'cause he was afraid I'd beat the heck out of him. And I would've, too. Anyway, the strongest picture was of him towering over me, yelling at me, and then kicking me to make his point.

"He'd holler at the top of his lungs to scare the heck out of me, telling me that if I didn't stop acting like a worthless little kid—as he called me—the neighbors would never have any respect for me. And then he'd kick me and say, 'That's for you to remember what I said.'"

Jimmy continues his self-analysis, but looks to his friend for some assistance. Jimmy's therapist had told him that when he began thinking about his own thoughts and feelings, it would be very easy to distort what actually happened. Fortunately, Jimmy had gotten into therapy because he saw that Eddie, who had already been in therapy for some time, had completed a lot of his own healing.

Jimmy asks, "Hey, help me out here, will you? From the way I reacted a few minutes ago with Jack, what beliefs do you think I had about myself?"

Eddie eagerly responds, "Well, for beginners, Jimmy, when you reacted that way you must have had the belief that you were still a powerless, weak little throwaway kid like your dad told you. Do you really and consciously believe that now?"

"No, of course not."

"Then," continues Eddie, "if you were to pretend to be a big brother to 'little Jimmy,' who was acting out his rage through you as an adult a few minutes ago, what would you want to say to him to make him feel better? Is there any wisdom you would give him?"

"Yeah, sure. First I'd tell little Jimmy that this experience will not last forever. . . and that he is not a 'disposable kid' but one of God's special people . . . that he just got stuck with a crippled family during his child-hood . . . and that when he grows up he doesn't have to let these memo-ries cripple him . . . that his old man was a drunk with his own pathetic self-image and absolutely no self-esteem . . . and that although his old man was bigger than he was then, little Jimmy doesn't need to take on his rotten self-image and lack of self-esteem. Lastly, I guess I'd tell him that it's really his old man's problem, not his, because he didn't ever do any-thing overtly wrong to hurt anyone else or to make his family look bad—kids just do kid stuff and get into trouble. His dad overreacted to what he was doing just growing up as a normal kid."

Jimmy lets out a long, deep breath, looks Eddie in the eye, and asks, "How was that?"

"Jimmy," exclaims Eddie, "that was terrific. Now repeat to yourself the most meaningful statements of belief that you told little Jimmy: 'I'm not a worthless kid but a special child of God. Kids make mistakes, and that's part of growing up. My dad's problems aren't my problems. I am not the same person my dad was, and I don't have to react like he did. And most important, I'm my own person now. I can *decide* in each situ-ation of my life how I want to react.'

"That's what you said to little Jimmy. There was a lot of wisdom in those words. So the next time Jack comes by and says something, just live in that moment. Listen to his words closely, be in touch with your body, be aware of your emotions, and listen to your own mind-talk words and pictures. Then respond to Jack like you'd want to as a mature, emotion-ally stable adult. Just like you'd tell little Jimmy to do."

Eddie winks and says, "That will be $150 for your 50-minute therapy hour, and it's time to go back to work."

What emotional issues do you think were evoked for Jimmy when the supervisor talked to him? Remember, at the time Jimmy wasn't reacting to the supervisor but to the "mind-pictures" of his father shouting, be-rating, and physically abusing him. Probably his reaction was motivated by physical *fear* of being kicked, *humiliation and victimization* from be-ing corrected in front of other people, *loathing* for the misuse of author-ity, *helplessness* when Jack stood over him, *worthlessness* for placing himself in a vulnerable situation, and probably much more. The situation did not warrant Jimmy's reaction, a reaction that left him dazed, tense, and stressed out. All too often such stress related to employment situations has its real origins in the childhood of the adult.

Living consciously in the moment is essential for emotional and social healing and for progressing on the spiritual path. It is indispensable for alcoholic recovery and healing co-dependency, and mandatory for over-coming violence in the home, whether spousal abuse, child abuse, self-abuse, or the destruction of property as an outlet for rage. Living consciously in the moment is as important for spiritual growth as it is for overcoming bad habits, negative mind-talk, violent mind–video clips, or any other form of negative response.

Mindful living puts depth into each intimate moment we share with friends and loved ones. It allows us to be fully present and emotionally available to ourselves and those around us when we are in need or when they just want to share their thoughts. To live consciously in the moment is to embrace life, feeling each breath we take and breathing in the full reality each moment has to offer.

6

Overcoming Erroneous Beliefs

The fundamentals of this chapter involve *will, consciousness,* and *living consciously in the moment.* All three are critical in the process of removing our erroneous beliefs and overcoming our emotional issues. We cannot learn to accept ourselves—let alone fully love ourselves—if we have not begun to heal our emotional wounds and replace faulty beliefs about ourselves with constructive, healthy ones.

Before discussing the practical steps needed to overcome erroneous beliefs, let's examine more closely how the mind creates and harbors its beliefs.

THE TWO LEVELS OF THE MIND

The energy the mind uses and manipulates has been called by some "universe energy." Universe energy, being nonphysical, is limited by neither time nor the three dimensions. It is fully manipulated by *both levels of our mind,* the conscious and the subconscious. Through conscious use of "will-commands," our conscious mind can outform (manifest or bring into existence) what we consciously command and affirm to come into our lives. On the other hand, the subconscious mind, which is blind to any reality outside itself, works continuously to outform *what it believes we need.*

Universe energy and its manipulation by the mind are the supporting principles for the development of the Christian metaphysical movement that began in the last half of the 1800s in Europe and the United States. Charles and Myrtle Fillmore founded Unity, Ernest Holmes founded the Church of Religious Science, and Mary Baker Eddy founded The Church of Christ Scientist, to give some leading examples.

The Conscious Mind

The conscious mind is the reasoning part of our mind that uses input from the present moment and past experience to make decisions. Using our will, we can consciously and intentionally examine our prior experiences to see which ones fit the current situation—using the wisdom we have on hand. We end up with a list of options, consciously select the best choice, and then use our will to take action.

The Subconscious Mind

The subconscious mind is the "logical" part of our mind. Like the conscious mind, it uses interpretations of prior situations, along with beliefs based on those interpretations, to decide what to bring into manifestation. However, its interpretations are arrived at in a very different way than those made by the conscious mind. Unlike the conscious mind, it doesn't have the ability to compare and contrast its beliefs or extrapolate data from the past and apply it in new ways to fit with the current situation. It is linear and procedural rather than inventive and exploratory.

The subconscious mind does not use reason. It equates its beliefs with truth and it will faithfully and ploddingly outform only according to the beliefs it has on hand, even if they are wildly inaccurate.

Simply removing old beliefs from the archives of our mind is not sufficient to correct our erroneous beliefs. The subconscious mind will continue to hunt for related and similar beliefs to guide our actions, just like a dedicated archivist would. Instead, core beliefs must be removed by being reinterpreted in light of new experience. These new interpretations must be repeatedly imprinted so they become embedded and operant at all times.

This situation is similar to using old software. There may not be anything wrong with the old software for handling old situations, but an upgrade is needed for new situations. Healing is all about removing old interpretations and beliefs and installing new ones. But it takes consciously applying our will, making decisions, and taking action to do this. It is not a passive process. Any vacillation on the part of the conscious mind will be interpreted by the subconscious mind as a signal to continue doing business as usual.

Have you ever noticed that all the efforts of successful people seem to be focused and directed? That is, all of their energies are working for them. Successful people usually have consistent, accurate beliefs and interpretations of past experiences. Few conflicting beliefs get in the way of their course in life. Their lives are integrated because beliefs and interpretations of the logical, subconscious mind and the reasoning, conscious mind are congruent, which allows the two aspects of the mind to work together harmoniously and productively.

On the other hand, we have seen many people—perhaps ourselves as well—who have had great difficulty moving ahead in life. Their progress is inconsistent—sometimes they surge ahead, sometimes they stand still, and at times they race backwards. Their lives are fragmented. Why is that? Because their subconscious and conscious minds are not working together, and often are working against each other. The beliefs of the subconscious mind do not support the decisions and actions of the conscious mind.

For example, a young woman was accepted at a local college to train to become a teacher, something she had always dreamed about and yearned for. She worked hard in school and got good grades, but in her second year she fell in love, became pregnant, and dropped out of school. Some people would say it was just one of those things that couldn't be helped. Yet many of her friends also fell in love and had lovers, but didn't get pregnant. Why?

What happened was not a simple slip-up in birth control; the young woman's subconscious mind was not supporting her decisions. Her subconscious mind was indoctrinated by her mother, who had casually but many times said as this young woman was growing up, "Women are the ones who carry the baby. We don't have a choice. When you fall in love, you get pregnant." Although this young woman didn't consciously accept what her mother had said, she did not refute or disbelieve it either.

We all are looking for success—to be in the flow of life, to have one success follow another and disappointments give way to more promising opportunities. But not all of us have experienced this wonderful flow. Why do some people continue to fail at what they attempt, even though their circumstances are positive and the outcomes are potentially good?

Remember that our subconscious mind is very simplistic. In a linear fashion, it produces good results when our beliefs are constructive, and difficulties and suffering when our beliefs are erroneous. You got pain and sufferin' in your life? Then somewhere in your mind is a set of erroneous beliefs operating like a defective software program.

Unhealthy beliefs held in the subconscious mind will continue to create problems until we consciously use our will to override those beliefs.

INDOCTRINATION

The programming of beliefs—what we call indoctrination—occurs in various ways in the conscious mind and in the subconscious mind:

1. *Conditioning* takes place with repeated exposure to learning situations over many years, from the time the child is in the womb until she leaves home. Subtle but constant indoctrination over a period of eighteen to twenty years can make a permanent, almost indelible imprint upon the mind of the child. When low-level indoctrination is reinforced by highly emotional incidents, either positive or negative, the

imprinted beliefs become rules for living inscribed almost as permanently as epitaphs chiseled in granite.

2. Indoctrination also occurs in *direct transference of beliefs*. The incidents of ordinary life provide all the occasions necessary to teach family traditions, biases, bigotries, loyalties, commitments, values, and more. Parents and other family members constantly tell children what to believe and what not to believe. In addition, religious leaders, teachers, and other authority figures transfer their beliefs to children.

3. Another powerful form of indoctrination occurs when we take *vows*. That is, what we are told is so convincingly in line with our beliefs that we adopt the new beliefs and incorporate them into a kind of vow that molds our future thoughts, words, and actions. Religious orders and military orders take vows. These can have a powerful karmic effect in our current life. Vows of poverty, chastity, silence, obedience, loyalty, eternal love, vengeance, servitude and indenture, and many more have an enormous amount of residual energy, unless they are broken with as much power and intention as was used when they were entered into.

4. Parents and other authority figures indoctrinate children through their *interpretations of events and situations*. Also, when parents remain silent, the interpretation is left to the child, whose interpretation may be far from realistic.

The erroneous beliefs that we devised about ourselves and our relationship to others are often the most insidious ones to remove. As an example, a young girl who lost both parents in a tragic fire that burned down their home devised beliefs about abandonment. Even though she was immediately adopted into the loving care of her aunt and uncle, she always harbored a fear of being left. She was both religious and spiritually developed, but this emotional issue haunted her for many, many years and had a powerful effect upon her relationships with parental figures, authority figures, and eventually a spouse. Her beliefs about abandonment were removed and replaced by beliefs of security only after she received traditional psychotherapeutic counseling and, later, spiritual clearings and healing.

Deep, erroneous beliefs about abandonment may also occur in a family situation where the child is told that he is worthless and that the parent had never wanted him to be born and wished he were gone. Emotional abandonment, rejection, and worthlessness get imprinted, leaving little room for another interpretation. These erroneous beliefs will haunt that adult until they are erased and replaced with healthy ones.

Children are easily susceptible to all forms of indoctrination whether in the form of healthy, constructive beliefs or erroneous, destructive beliefs. All it takes is persistent and consistent application of indoctrination techniques.

Children are so susceptible simply because they don't have enough experience and wisdom to challenge the beliefs they are given or to form their own correct interpretations and conclusions about events and situations. Further, children do not have the consciousness to be aware that it is okay to have differences of belief. When they do challenge what they are told to believe, they are often overruled by the authority figure. Lastly, until early adulthood, children usually have not developed their faculty of will, so they are unable to consciously choose a set of beliefs that can guide them more constructively than those given to them by their parents or other authority figures.

WHY ERRONEOUS BELIEFS ARE SO HARD TO REMOVE

Both levels of the mind can be filled with erroneous or inconsistent beliefs. However, whereas erroneous subconscious beliefs are difficult to remove and replace, erroneous beliefs of the conscious mind are relatively easy to remove and replace. For example, a businesswoman who eventually became successful had to remove the obviously erroneous conscious belief that women aren't tough enough to be in business and make it, which she had heard as a child.

The beliefs of the subconscious mind are difficult to uproot because they are invisible to our conscious mind. Unless we become aware of them, we cannot make direct, conscious decisions about whether to keep them or remove them. *It is only by the evidence of unhappy living that we know we have erroneous beliefs in our subconscious mind.*

The businesswoman who removed the erroneous conscious belief that women aren't tough enough to make it in business also had to struggle with many erroneous subconscious beliefs that caused her a lot of grief in her career before she became successful. Perhaps the liabilities list in her business plan should have included a list of psychological as well as financial liabilities. She then would have had a guide for looking back to her childhood to find that the incessant indoctrination she received from her domineering, belittling father and from her submissive, suffering mother provided a system of erroneous subconscious beliefs she would have to overcome that would be as challenging to deal with as the unsalable inventory she received with the business she bought.

When we are not successful, when we are consistently unhappy and unsatisfied, that is the time to look deep within ourselves and ask "Why?" With help, the answers can be discovered quickly, though the ultimate solutions may take weeks and months, depending on the method of healing that is used.

REMOVING AND REPLACING ERRONEOUS BELIEFS

Many of us are unfortunately very comfortable with our erroneous beliefs. We have great difficulty removing them and replacing them with beliefs that at first seem foreign and just weird. It is no wonder that it has taken some of us many years to rid ourselves of our raging co-dependency. It took years to learn it and was later reinforced by spouses, bosses, neighbors, and friends.

It took me forty-plus years of inconsistency, relationship pain, anguish in careers, and sorrow with children, parents, spouses, and lovers to finally wake up and say, "Hey! Something's not working in my life! I gotta do something different to keep living, or I'll die. What can I do differently? What should I do differently? Where do I begin?"

To initiate healing, we must first *feel the pain* (sorrow, anguish, rejection, guilt, resentment, bitterness, rage, worthlessness, and hopelessness) in our life as it exists in the moment. Second, we have to *acknowledge that the pain exists.* If we don't feel the pain, we surely aren't ready to change our harmful beliefs. When we finally do feel the pain of our life, we must consciously and authentically desire and need to remove that pain. Pain in our life is a message that says, "The world is not in agreement with what you believe to be true."

Since we cannot change what is outside of ourselves, the only thing we can change is what is on the inside: our beliefs. Since what we believe is causing us pain and anguish and sorrow, those beliefs must simply be wrong. Now is the time to begin the process of removing our erroneous beliefs, replacing them with healthy, constructive beliefs about ourselves and our relationship with others. But we must consciously and intentionally *will* to do so!

Until we consciously *will* to replace our erroneous beliefs, they will continue to run like a computer with flawed software. No matter how much new input is given, the outcomes will not be successful. We must take action to rewrite our subconscious set of beliefs in order to produce outcomes that work. *If we only remove them but do not fill in the space in our mind with positive beliefs, the old ones will reappear.*

Replacing erroneous beliefs is very important because once the subconscious mind is imprinted with a belief, the imprint will remain there even if the conscious mind does not agree with that old belief. As an example, let us use the racially biased statement "Blacks are inferior to whites." If we consciously remove the old belief by saying, "I just don't believe that anymore," but do not imprint a new belief over the old one, the old belief will show up when our mind searches for information and beliefs about the differences between the races. We must imprint a new belief, such as: "Each person is better at some things and worse at others; that has nothing to do with being black or white." Then, when the mind searches for information about the racial differences, it will find the belief that there are differences *and* similarities, but they don't signify inferiority or superiority.

Evidence of Partial Success

Partial success in removing erroneous beliefs is evident when we experience fleeting periods of happiness and brief episodes of success. Unhappiness may return, but with the hope that happiness will also come again. Partial success occurs when erroneous beliefs have been removed but not replaced with healthy beliefs, and/or when only some erroneous beliefs have been removed and replaced with healthy beliefs.

Consciousness of this state of fleeting happiness is very important. Being conscious of our happiness, even if it lasts only for a few moments, allows us to consciously and willfully push our spiritual growth forward. It urges us to acknowledge, "Hey, wow! I was happy for a little while. I must have done something right." Then ask:

1. What did I do differently that brought about this brief period of happiness? What new belief did I have that supported this brief period of happiness?
2. What did I do (or not do) that ended this brief period of happiness? What old belief did I revert to that ended my happiness?

At this point in our progress, it is important to identify the beliefs that support our newfound happiness, because doing so will reveal the congruence and agreement between our conscious mind and our subconscious mind. We want this band of agreement and congruence to broaden and deepen so that every moment of our life is filled with success and happiness. On the other hand, if we become morose and obsess about our failure, we are just reinforcing our old erroneous beliefs as being logically correct.

On our spiritual journey, we will discover many positive statements we were taught that do not produce good results because of our conflicting beliefs. For instance, prayer is often only partially productive because somewhere in our subconscious mind are beliefs that impede or stop the flow of energy initiated by our prayers. That is, what we reasonably and consciously want and pray for, our unconscious mind logically believes will not occur. This is because our past experience tells us that prayer is more ceremonial than effective since people rarely get what they pray for. Therefore, the subconscious mind believes that prayer will not work.

Ultimately, we need to examine our conflicting beliefs about God. Is God a God of wrath and vengeance or a God of love and forgiveness? This is a basic theological quandary many people suffer with but do not explore. Discovering what the Creator is really about is central to our spiritual journey and essential for our emotional healing.

TAKING ACTION TO HEAL OURSELVES

I have found that I do not become motivated to begin the healing process until the pain outweighs the desire to continue living as I do. When I am motivated, taking the following steps is very simple:

1. Awareness of pain or unhappiness. It's useful to describe exactly what you feel. Pain may take the form of anguish, resentment, anger, depression, rage, jealousy, hostility, bitterness, perennial negative think-

ing, pessimism, hypercriticalness, and numerous other states.

2. An evaluation of the pain and unhappiness. For example, "Man, I can't stand feeling this angry all the time. I don't like how unhappy I feel. I know that if I don't make some changes, I'll either end up on drugs or in a mental hospital, my body will self-destruct from a heart attack, or I'll get cancer or some other disease."

3. A motivation to change. "There is no happiness in my life anymore. I need to change how I'm living, feeling, and thinking."

4. A decision to change. "I've definitely decided to change how I am living."

5. Initiation of action. "I made an appointment with a therapist who was recommended to me. She can see me this afternoon."

6. A commitment to change. "I'm going to see this change through for sure. I'm committed to living more happily, easily, and peacefully, and I'm not going to get off this path of healing until I'm done."

7. A continuing consciousness of thought and emotions. "I must live in each moment. I know now that it is essential to be fully aware of the thoughts I am thinking and the emotions I am feeling in order to relate my healing with every minute, and to relate every minute of my life to my healing."

No amount of wanting to be healed will heal us until we *sincerely and willfully* command all the resources of the universe and our mind to begin the healing process. I can remember shouting at the top of my lungs to God, to all of His spiritual helpers, and to all levels of my mind, "God and all your universe, help me to heal all levels of my being—my personality, my mind, my injured memories, and my body! I command all levels of my mind to begin the healing process, to heal my emotional injuries, my co-dependency, and any mental processes and beliefs that are causing pain in the way I live!"

We must give this command as much energy as is held in the emotional injuries locked up in our most powerful traumatic memories. We must powerfully *will* our conscious mind and subconscious mind to begin the process.

Cutting Our Losses

Healing the way we live and think through removing and replacing our erroneous beliefs is neither easy nor painless. It is difficult to change habits of living and thinking that have been unconscious and routine. Sometimes healing means we have to end relationships because other people want us to remain as we are—either dependent and weak so we rely solely upon them, or co-dependent so we continue to meet their needs without caring for ourselves.

Sometimes healing means stopping self-destructive habits such as alcohol abuse, drug abuse, picking fights, playing friends or family members against each other, indulging in self-pity, and so on. Sometimes healing means we have to stop guarding our painful childhood memories, overeating, going on binges, overspending, or overextending ourselves.

Healing means taking time to be with ourselves, alone, in thoughtful, loving consciousness, so we can look within and see where the pain comes from that propels us to do the things that hurt us.

GOALS OF HEALING

1. Living consciously in the moment; taking just one day at a time.
2. Learning to examine a situation, our body's tension, our emotions, and our thoughts before reacting.
3. Becoming aware that wherever there is negative mind-talk and negative mind-pictures there is a need for healing.
4. Working through our personal problems as they arise.
5. Reinterpreting and reframing negative emotion-filled memories.
6. Replacing erroneous beliefs about ourselves with healthy beliefs.
7. Replacing negative mind-talk and pictures with healthy mind-talk and pictures.

8. Gaining wisdom from negative emotion-filled memories.
9. Releasing the emotional energy locked in the incomplete developmental memory of our child within; and as an adult, continuing the broken development that was interrupted in childhood.
10. Being *centered* in the moment—neither in the past nor the future.
11. Being *grounded* in reality—neither unrealistic nor too pragmatic.
12. Being *balanced* in emotions—neither numb nor frenetic.

For us, as human beings on a semi-uncivilized planet, healing and our spiritual journey are synonymous. Healing is the process of using all the errors and distorted beliefs of material life to become spiritually wise and mature in the truths that govern all relationships in the universe. Healing is learning to live consciously in each moment so that eventually we can live in the consciousness of the Eternal Now.

Healing is essential for progress upon our spiritual journey, because a will that governs and directs a mind that is out of balance will bring into existence a life that is misdirected and chaotic. But a will that governs a mended mind can bring into existence a life that is loving, forgiving, kind, gentle, peaceful, and productive for ourselves and others.

7

Getting to Forgiveness

One of the simplest but most difficult acts of love and healing we can do in a relationship is to forgive. Forgiving provides us with a transformative understanding of our tormentors. We come to see them as not beneath us but as our teachers, who bring our weaknesses to our attention. Without them we would never learn how we need to grow spiritually.

The ability to completely forgive also validates our emotional and spiritual growth. It is the verification of the reality of our healing and our commitment to being love(ing)—i.e., being an embodiment of love (see chapter 10)—expressed as a belief of our conscious and subconscious minds. The benefits of complete forgiveness are enormous. As forgiveness moves into our lives, it is accompanied by fruits of the spirit such as peace, tolerance, patience, forbearance, understanding, and love, including love for ourselves.

Forgiveness can be defined as:
- The application of a higher model of loving consciousness in our relationships, either with ourselves or with others.
- The experience of love in its most active and effective form.
- The release of old beliefs and their energy and the acceptance of new beliefs and their energy.

• Evidence of profound transformation of anger into love, and resentment and spite into acceptance and appreciation.

THE PROFUNDITY OF FORGIVENESS

There is no evidence more expressive of our intent to achieve Master Consciousness than our sincere forgiveness of those who have wronged us. The conscious act of sincere forgiveness has profound implications for our participation in sacred relationships and for our soul's growth. It is the product of an almost inexplicable awakening in us of a new level of spiritual maturity that transforms our self-pity and emotional pain into appreciation for the actions of the person we forgive.

This awakening is our conscious realization that our bruised ego and raw emotions are evidence of *our need* for growth. We come to see that it was not the antagonist who hurt us; the antagonist merely *uncovered* our hurt emotions! In that reflective moment, we come to understand that the issue is not solely the other person, but our relationship to our own wounds.

Forgiveness is the final result of a mysterious, Master-like "Aha!" realization in the depths of our being that the person who we once saw as our nemesis has now become our salvation by virtue of presenting us with evidence of our spiritual weakness. The definition of the word "nemesis" provides us with further insight into this transformation:

Nemesis 1. the Greek goddess of retributive justice, or vengeance.
2. (a) just punishment; retribution. (b) one who imposes retribution.
3. anyone or anything by which, it seems, we must inevitably be defeated or frustrated.

In Greek mythology, Nemesis is the avenger of wrongs, righting the wrongs that come into our lives. In the act of forgiveness, our nemesis, our tormentor and persecutor, is the one who points out our emotional issues and our spiritual weaknesses.

It is fitting that the antonym for "nemesis" is "salvation." Only when we consciously and sincerely appreciate our antagonists can they make us aware of our weaknesses and turn them into strengths, thus becoming the salvation in our spiritual growth.

Eventually, the exercise of forgiveness will teach us to anticipate new situations in which people may persecute us. When similar situations arise, we can use that awareness to immediately see the situation for what it is: an opportunity to disclose how we need to grow spiritually. We accept our nemesis as our teacher in that moment and do not react emotionally. Then we have become the master of that moment and Master Teacher of our own spiritual education. This is evidence of real progress toward conscious living.

When another hurtful situation occurs, we can say to ourselves, "Aha! Looks like I get to find out if I have more spiritual homework to do. I look forward to understanding why this situation came into my life. Now I can accept it as a challenge for spiritual growth. *Thank you!*"

For those of us involved in conscious and intentional relationships, our partner is the safest person to be our nemesis and conscious mirror. We can anticipate that our partner will bring up all of our hidden emotional baggage, push our buttons, get our goat, and reveal our social and personal issues in public—and we love them for it! But our sacred relationship partner is also our salvation, for with unconditional love she can ask, "Why are you reacting so emotionally to what I said?" and "How can I help you process your emotional pain that caused you to react as you did?"

Unstoppable love, forgiveness, understanding, joy, and appreciation are the primary ingredients that people in sacred relationships use every day to move through their issues. Anticipating the emotional work that we may need to do and saying "Thank you!" are essential for maintaining sacred relationships.

WHY FORGIVE?

Spiritual Growth

We grow spiritually when we forgive sincerely. Sincere forgiveness is experiential evidence that validates spiritual growth. It is evidence of a new consciousness and new beliefs.

Soul Growth

Forgiving is a moral choice, and right moral choices add weight to our soul. Further, initiating forgiveness before it is requested of us also adds weight to our soul. It becomes the proactive expression of Master Consciousness that seeks to right wrongs, straighten the path, and smooth the way for others and ourselves.

Peace of Mind

Forgiveness allows us to achieve peace of mind, peace in our relationship with ourselves, and peace in social and work relationships. Some would equate peace of mind with being happy or content with life.

Undoing Karma

For those of you concerned about karma (what "comes around"), remember that forgiving *stops* karma no matter when it began, and that loving others even when they do wrong to us *prevents* karma. Forgiving is a transcendent act of love—evidence of spiritual ascendancy that releases karma from prior lifetimes. Genuine, earnest forgiveness eliminates all karma. Forgiving past-life injustices eliminates preexisting karma; forgiving present-life injustices prevents karma in this lifetime.

Failure to Forgive Creates Emotional Blocks

On the other hand, failure to forgive when we know forgiveness is needed freezes us emotionally and creates an emotional blockage. The negative emotional energy in our subconscious mind will continue to exist as a latent and potent force to energize our erroneous beliefs, which will manifest themselves in our conscious life, to be relived again in this lifetime or the next. We will have no peace in our mind as long as we cannot forgive.

WHAT TO FORGIVE

What we forgive is not important. We don't forgive a "what," we forgive a person.

When facing someone who has injured us, it is very important to forgive the *person*, not the injury. "I forgive you for what you did. If you had been living consciously in the moment, I am sure you would not have done what you did."

Forgive whoever has hurt you and anyone you have negative thoughts about. *Forgive. Learn to love the person, not their actions.* Every one of us has done something to hurt others. We need their forgiveness as much as they need ours.

WHO BENEFITS FROM FORGIVING?

Ultimately, forgiveness is just for ourselves. To forgive others for their sake alone is condescending, egoistic, and arrogant and can cause further separation between us and them. Though it is helpful to forgive other people and to help them work through their own emotional issues about a shared event or incident, we do it ultimately for ourselves.

Forgiveness can be done cleanly, clearly, and completely alone, without anyone else involved. Whether or not the other person is able to receive our forgiveness is not important. If we offer authentic forgiveness and someone rejects it, we still benefit. If they are receptive to our forgiveness, then we have both grown spiritually.

Sincerely offered forgiveness and sincerely received forgiveness occur within the heart and mind. It is the experience of accepting a new belief about our relationship to the other person and to ourselves. This is transformation in its truest and most sincere form.

WHEN DO WE FORGIVE AND HOW OFTEN?

We need to forgive when we feel emotionally injured, indignant, insulted, offended, or hurt. If we are not living consciously in the moment, we may instead react with embarrassment, guilt, shame, or anger. If such reactions continue to escalate, we may "lose it" and act out our negative emotions verbally and physically.

To prevent this result, forgiveness is needed immediately after we feel our body tense up, our pulse rise, and our breathing quicken, even while the actual harm is being done. *Negative emotional energy is evidence that forgiveness is needed now.* Absence of negative emotional energy is evidence that forgiveness is not needed at the time or would be ineffectual.

FORGIVENESS AND TOXIC MEMORIES

Every time the *thought* of a person or the *memory* of their actions causes us to become emotionally upset, it is time to forgive again. Toxic memories, filled with the energy of toxic emotions such as anger, resentment, and bitterness, leave telltale evidence of their presence in our body, such as a tight brow, faster heartbeat, sweaty palms, tightness in the abdomen, faster breathing, thoughts of revenge or regret, and so on. Memories that cause our bodies to react this way and make our emotions run wild are toxic to our physical well-being and our mental and emotional health.

Although the event that set the memory in place is in the past, the energy in the toxic memory causes us, in the present, to have the same reactions and emotions, pain, and anguish as during the actual event, whether that was six minutes or sixty years ago. *It is the bottled-up emotional energy in the memory that causes the pain.*

Every toxic memory must be forgiven again and again until the memory of the injury or act of injustice no longer carries any emotional energy. This is what Jesus meant when he said we must forgive seventy times seven, if necessary (Matt. 18:22–23). Toxic memories can make our heart pound, palms sweat, and brow tighten even after ten, twenty, thirty, forty, or fifty years. I know several people who, even after sixty years, harbor toxic memories that still affect their intimate relationships and their physical and mental health.

Healing Toxic Memories

Toxic memories are tough to get rid of. If you find you cannot forgive easily, try using healing therapies and techniques. Conversely, if you started with healing techniques and therapies and they have not been successful, then begin the process of forgiving. *Willing* to forgive initiates the process. *Healing begins in our mind when our will initiates forgiveness.* The conscious mind must forgive over and over again until the subconscious mind is fully impressed with our intent for it to release the energy it holds in that memory. The conscious mind must work to reframe and reinterpret the incident(s) that created the toxic memories, formulate new beliefs about those incidents, and then put energy into the process so the new beliefs stay in place.

Dealing with Engrams

If peace of mind is hard to achieve, several things may be occurring. As long as there remain unforgiven injuries in our early history, it is likely that some action of another person will remind us of a similar earlier incident and we will become as emotionally upset as we did back then. Thus we become aware of another situation that needs to be forgiven. Some therapists call these chains of memories *engrams.*

We can trace this line of pain in the chronology of our life. The last incident that initiated a significant negative emotional reaction is a place to start. Forgive the person and her actions. When that is done, recall an earlier incident that reminds you of the most recent one. Forgive that person and his actions. Keep repeating this process until you can remember no earlier incidents that remind you of what happened most recently.

The next step is to take the emotional energy out of the toxic memories by using one or several energy-release techniques. By releasing the energy from the earliest memory, we can break the chain leading to the most recent painful incident.

WHEN IS FORGIVENESS COMPLETE?

Forgiveness is complete when the negative emotional energy in a memory no longer exists. *You will know this process is complete when you have a memory or thought of the old incident or person and you fail to get upset or angry.* All that remains is a veiled image of the old memory without any negative energy. When forgiveness is complete, old, hurtful memories fade from being solid, moving, Technicolor, emotion-filled "video clips" to shadowy, black/gray/white still-frame pictures, vague images of what used to be. The memory remains, but the repressed emotional energy is gone.

A caution: Just because people do not feel their rage about a prior traumatic situation does not mean it is gone. Many adults have a lot of repressed anger, hate, and rage that originated in their childhood. A tip-off that there is unresolved anger or rage is the presence of periodic and episodic depression. When complete forgiveness has occurred, no residual emotional energy is locked in toxic memories. There may still be memories, but no energy is left in them to cause physical and emotional stress, tension symptoms, or depression. Then the memories are no longer toxic.

HOW TO FORGIVE

Approach 1: Will to Forgive by Being Love(ing)

The goal in this approach is to move into Master Consciousness: *being love(ing)*. Since the necessity for forgiveness is so intimately linked to our emotional energy, we need to become peaceful and emotionally balanced in order to forgive effectively. Meditation practices accomplish this well.

• Begin by getting into a relaxed physical position.

- Release tension from your muscles.
- Breathe deeply from your abdomen.
- Visualize the release of all body stress and tension through your breath.
- Now begin to feel peaceful and *be love(ing)*. Come to rest in the space of *peace, acceptance,* and *appreciation* of all that is, as it is, where it is.
- Say aloud, "I align my *intent to forgive* with the Master Consciousness of *being love(ing)*."
- Now quiet your thoughts and move into a state of meditative stillness.

In this state of consciousness, we can begin to exercise our *will to be love(ing)*. It is then possible to almost instantaneously forgive—completely.

If you feel any resistance to forgiving, ask your Guardian Angel and celestial guides and teachers to help you co-creatively move into the full and receptive consciousness of forgiveness. If you are still unable to move yourself into forgiveness, take willful action. Begin by removing erroneous beliefs and installing constructive and healthy beliefs about the person(s) to be forgiven, and remove all the surrounding negative energy.

The following exercise of rewriting stubborn erroneous beliefs may also help. It is said that repetition is the wheel that makes a rut for a new habit. In this exercise, you can use the process of repetition constructively to form healthy habits and new beliefs:

- Will to find and discover love in the person(s) to be forgiven. Ask yourself, "How would the Master love these, his spiritual children?"
- Will to forgive them, even though your heart may not be convinced it is the thing you would really like to do.
- Speak your forgiveness aloud. Listen to your words. The intent is not just to *want* to forgive them but to *will* to forgive them.
- Say, "I *will* to love. I *will* to forgive." And, "I love! I forgive!"
- Write this down, then read it aloud.
- Ask your Guardian Angel for help.

Approach 2: Forgive Through Control of Thinking

How much control do we have over our thinking? More than we think!

Try this: When painful thoughts or memories start running through your mind, say aloud, with emphasis, "I don't want to think about that!" Emphasis puts energy into a command. The energy enables the command to be stored.

If those thoughts arise again and you don't want to think about them, say aloud, again with emphasis, *"I don't want to think about that!"* Every time the memories come up, say your command again. Eventually, the energy you put into the command will become greater than the energy that holds the old memory in place.

As you are energizing the commands to stop thinking about the old memories, forgiving simultaneously removes energy from the toxic memories. The complete command is now, "I don't want to think about (incident)! I forgive (person's name) and release all negative energy from these memories!" While you are giving energy to new, healthy, healing commands, you are turning toxic memories into plain, ordinary vanilla memories.

Those of us who have toxic memories running loose in our minds can take command of our minds first by *willing* to reclaim the land of our thoughts, then by digging out the weeds of old thoughts and memories, and finally by planting a new, productive garden of healthy, healing thoughts.

Where to start? Decide what thoughts you want in your mind; decide what thoughts you don't want in your mind. Make lists of these thoughts. Yes, really—make written lists. Work on them. Carry the lists with you. Then visually imagine dumping out old thoughts and energy in the amount that you can handle, and bring in new thoughts and energy in the amount you can handle. It takes time; proceed slowly. Again, dump out hurtful thoughts and memories only as fast as you can handle, then pull in caring, appreciative, and loving thoughts only in amounts that do not overwhelm you. It works!

Approach 3: Visualize the Act as Separate from the Person

Begin by seeing the act as separate from the person. *The person is not the act, and the act is not the person.* This objective perspective is similar to how mature adults deal with children. We love the child but do not approve of their misguided actions. It's okay to attach hostile feelings to the ill treatment someone gave to you, but not to the person or to their worth.

Yes, it's hard to do, but it can be done. For instance, if the act is rude, that does not mean the person is rude. It may mean he or she just doesn't know any better. Remember that each of us is always doing the best we can at any given time.

This must be how Masters view errant people. Surely they know the "big picture," and know, too, that if people who do unethical or immoral acts knew the big picture, they wouldn't act as they do. When we take on the Master's perspective, we too can see errant adults as spiritual children and forgive them because they really don't know what they are doing in the big scheme of the universe.

FORGIVING OURSELVES

Now that we have considered forgiveness of others, let's look at what is perhaps the toughest act of forgiveness: forgiving ourselves.

Using the spiritual authority of our will, self-forgiveness requires that we step into the shoes of our higher consciousness, our Master Consciousness. Forgiving ourselves is not an exercise of a self-justifying ego but an action of our higher consciousness that views our lower consciousness and behavior as that of a stubborn, slow learner. We must have great detachment from our ego to accomplish this.

It is probably more difficult for us to forgive ourselves than to forgive others, especially if we tend to be perfectionists. But if we can forgive others, we can forgive ourselves.

Sometimes we agonize over making the same mistakes over and over again; we offend, injure, and emotionally torture our loved ones and our friends, not knowing why or how to stop. For a perfectionist, that is agony. Instead we need to see ourselves as growing, spiritual children striving to live in Master Consciousness but still prone to error. It is best to start by forgiving yourself a little at a time. Avoid expectations of perfection. See yourself as a spiritual, ethical, moral, and social child, not perfect but *becoming perfect.*

Even if you cannot speak the words with feeling, begin by saying, "I forgive you, (your own name)." Do it in the morning and again before going to sleep. Say it while looking into a mirror. It is very powerful to repeat this to yourself. If it is too difficult, begin by giving yourself permission to forgive yourself. Then try saying it again.

Examine your intent to forgive. Is it earnest and clear or is it stained by the need of the ego to simply relieve itself of guilt? *One of our intents in forgiving ourselves should be the realignment of our will to prevent us from causing injury again.* Sincere forgiveness, with true remorse and regret for what we did, is the practice of living consciously in the moment with the intent of changing our behavior.

Forgiving ourselves is a very important part of healing ourselves. Often, after we have healed our emotional injuries, we still need to do a lot of self-forgiveness.

In summary, continue to forgive yourself as you forgive others. Meditate to attain emotional peace and calm and then to raise your consciousness to the level of your spiritual Masters. Look for *a change in the emotional energy* in yourself. Look for *a change in the beliefs* you have about yourself. Look for *new energy, enthusiasm, and positivity* about yourself. These are good indications that your forgiveness work is effective.

RECEIVING FORGIVENESS

Entitlement to forgiveness is far more important than most people imagine. The principle of entitlement—of being entitled to *receive* and to *give,* to *love,* and to *forgive*—underlies all healthy relationships, including our relationship to God.

If we do not feel entitled to give or receive love or forgiveness *to or from ourselves,* how can we ever feel entitled to receive love or forgiveness *from others*? Conversely, if we do not feel entitled to give or receive love or forgiveness *to or from others,* how can we ever feel entitled to receive love or forgiveness *from ourselves*?

If we have disenfranchised and rejected ourselves, the task of learning to love and forgive ourselves is a mighty big one. It begins by being able to literally ask: "Am I entitled to receive love, any kind of love? Am I entitled to be forgiven for any of the things I think I did wrong in my life, whether it was a big wrong or a little wrong?" If you can answer yes to either of these questions, know that you are holding open the floodgates to receiving love and forgiveness in your life. When you feel entitled to receive the love of even a small puppy after forgetting to feed it before leaving for work in a hurry, then you can have access to feel and know all the love and forgiveness that fill the universe.

The point is that if you can give or receive love or forgiveness even a little bit, then you can have it all. God's pipelines of love and forgiveness have no valves or restrictions. They flow wide open all the time. The only limit to the amount of love we can receive is the self-imposed limit we place on our own acceptance of it.

BEING THANKFUL FOR FORGIVENESS

You might ask, "What can being thankful possibly have to do with being loved and forgiven?" Being thankful for forgiveness does several important things.

First, being thankful is a way of showing appreciation, a diminutive form of love.

Second, giving thanks puts energy into forgiveness so that the act of forgiveness has the necessary energy to stay in our mind to heal (replace) negative and destructive memories.

Third, being thankful provides a rite of completion in the process of forgiveness. It provides the final act of closure to a difficult task.

LOVING ACTION AFTER FORGIVING

What do you do if you see a child being chastised, berated, or beaten in the grocery store? It is an excellent choice to forgive the adult immediately, but in this example you also need to decide quickly whether more than forgiveness may be needed. Even if you say nothing but simply walk up and stand by them to stop the adult's unreasonable behavior, that may be enough. If you do not know what to do, ask yourself, "What would a Master do in this situation? What action would a Master take, here and now?" Then apply that action. If you do not have a Master to give you an example, you might ask yourself, "What would a loving, protective angel do in this situation?" And so on.

To forgive or be forgiven does not mean that we become impotent in our social, ethical, and moral life. Quite the contrary, it *empowers us to act in Master Consciousness* for the good of all concerned. Sometimes that means doing nothing; sometimes that may even mean stepping into harm's way.

Socializing with Those We've Forgiven

Be discerning, too, in socializing with those who have injured you. To be always forgiving does not mean that you have to socialize with the people who injured you. That may be an invitation to be injured by that person again. Just because we forgive people does not mean we have to be pals with them or like them. This is a form of loving action toward ourselves.

Responsibility for Our Actions

Being forgiven for our own wrongdoing does not mean we are no longer responsible for what we did. Likewise, forgiveness of others does not mean they are no longer accountable for their past actions. Forgiveness is attached to the value, acceptance, and appreciation of the person as another fallible child of God, not to their actions and the damage they caused.

Imagine life as a baseball season in the minor leagues. Our goal is to play as well as we can, commit as few errors as possible, and be chosen by major-league scouts. Yet some of us will commit too many errors trying to be "hot dog" players; others won't play to our capacity. Even though our errors will be forgiven, we can't escape the consequence that we won't be chosen for the majors. As the season comes to a close, there is no way to make up for all those errors. All we can do is play each remaining game as though it were the only game in the season and know we will be judged by our intent and performance in our last game. If in the end it's not good enough, we may be permitted to return to the minors next season and try again.

Forgiveness is necessary when we do not live in Master Consciousness in each moment, and when we have not consistently loved ourselves and others. Forgiveness is a profoundly transformative spiritual, intellectual, and emotional process, an experience of love-in-action motivated from a higher consciousness. In that higher consciousness, we will be able to forgive others and thank them for bringing a lesson of spiritual growth to us.

We must be able to know and feel forgiveness for others and ourselves before we can experience, feel, and *know* that we have been forgiven by God. We come to realize that God forgives us because He knows we are still in the process of learning how to live in sacred relationship.

8

Healing Co-Creatively

This chapter could be entitled "Self-Healing with Universal Energy" because cosmic law allows us to use our own mind to manipulate universal energy to heal ourselves. But using only our mind has an inherent flaw: Our mind will only outform what we desire based on our beliefs, which may be in error. Then our efforts to heal ourselves will be misguided. *Co-creative healing*, on the other hand, *involves the conscious and intentional invitation to spiritual beings of light*—whether deities, angels, or celestial guides and teachers—*to voluntarily participate with us in the healing process*. Spiritual beings of light are able to manipulate universe energy and manifest healing based on beliefs that are far more consistently aligned with the laws of God's universe of light and love than our own. With their participation, we can co-creatively heal what we alone cannot.

THE DAWNING OF THE CO-CREATIVE ERA

The last half of the 1800s and the first decade of the 1900s saw the sprouting of a profound new spiritual movement in the Western world. As mentioned before, this movement was shaped by the lives of Ernest Holmes (Church of Religious Science), Charles and Myrtle Fillmore (Unity), Mary

Baker Eddy (Church of Christ Scientist), Joseph Smith (Church of Jesus Christ of the Latter-Day Saints), Ellen White (Seventh-Day Adventists), Madame Blavatsky (Theosophy), and, later, Edgar Cayce (Association for Research and Enlightenment), Rudolf Steiner, William Sadler (*The Urantia Book* and Urantia Brotherhood), and many more. Each of these individuals had personal and conscious contact with beings of light and received metaphysical insights they later developed into innovative world-class teachings of light.

While today we can see that the celestial influence upon these leaders was unified in spirit, their individual expressions varied immensely. Some experienced waking visions once or several times. Some were spiritists who saw and conversed directly with spiritual beings, and some received revelatory information clairvoyantly. Some became outcasts of their religious communities; others founded their own spiritual movement, or greatly influenced existing religious institutions. All became involved in working directly with spiritual beings or influences, either consciously or unconsciously. The conscious, spiritually co-creative era had begun.

DIVISIONS OF THE HEALING ARTS

One of the chief interests of these early pioneers was healing. Three divisions of healing arts were greatly advanced through these new spiritual influences. These include the allopathic medical industry, naturopathy, and spiritual healing.

Today, the most widely known division of the healing arts is the allopathic healing therapies of general practice physicians and the allopathic surgeons and specialists who treat the hundreds of specialized parts of the human anatomy. The allopathic pharmaceutical industry is an integral part of this.

The second division consists of the naturopathic healing therapies. These have been handed down over centuries, but did not become organized or studied scientifically until this era. This tradition of healing quickly evolved into a holistic healing system to address the total physical, emotional, mental, and spiritual needs of people. Its approach is far broader than the allopathic approach because it takes into account the various energy systems of the body and strives to maintain the balance of the whole being of a person. Today naturopathy includes healing practices not recognized by the allopathic healing community, such as homeopathy, chiropractic, acupuncture, acupressure, therapeutic massage, and dozens more.

The third division is broadly called spiritual healing, which is composed of two branches. One branch involves the manipulation of universe energy by the mind, and does not involve anything spiritual to affect the desired healing. A better name for this type of healing is white magic. The word "white" is used because the intent of the manipulator is benign, positive, and constructive. The word "magic" is a misnomer, though, as there is no legerdemain, or sleight of hand, involved, but simply the use of mind and will to manipulate universe energy for specific outcomes.

The second branch of spiritual healing involves the co-creative participation of spiritual beings of light to manipulate universe energy for healing.

CO-CREATIVE SPIRITUAL HEALING

Co-creative healing involves the manipulation of universe energy by our mind and will, motivated by our conscious and intentional *invitation* to spiritual beings of light to help us manipulate that energy for healing. Because we know that we have erroneous beliefs and great gaps in our knowledge of how to use universe energy effectively, we ask these unseen spiritual helpers to direct the application of universe energy for right outcomes of healing. Our part is to initiate the healing process and then contribute where we can to the movement of healing energy.

We initiate the healing process by making a positive, proactive, co-creative statement. For example, the simplest co-creative command goes something like this: "Dear God and Angels of Healing, with your co-creative participation, I command universe energy to heal (_____)."

To ensure that the healing process and outcomes are spiritually, mentally, emotionally, and physically efficacious, we add qualifying clauses to the co-creative command. I always add *"for right and perfect outcomes"* and *"according to God's will."* This prevents my beliefs from limiting the form and extent of healing and ensures that right and perfect forms of healing are used, because I don't know if healing is the right and perfect outcome.

Co-creative spiritual healing puts us in the driver's seat to *initiate* the manipulation of universe energy, but gets us out of the way so those who are more adept can do the actual manipulation. In other words, we command the co-creative use of universe energy for the outcomes we perceive are needed, but allow for this process to be amended or aborted.

Co-creative spiritual healing is the most effective middle ground of spiritual healing. On one side is the use of ineffectual, will-less supplications to God, and on the other side is the use of ineffectual, egoistic, willful, and arrogant commands and demands to God. *We cannot effectively command God, angels, celestial teachers, helpers, or guides to do anything. We must invite them to participate with us.* If they decline the invitation, then no harm is done to either ourselves or the person we are praying for.

One reason that beings of light might decline our co-creative invitation is if our intention and our sincerity in relation to the purposes of the healing are not in full alignment with the good that would come from an answered invitation. We can expect that any prayer, co-creative command, or request that is for the benefit of our ego will not be fulfilled. This is true whether our intention is spoken or unspoken, conscious or unconscious.

My protection against this error is to add the qualifier, *"I ask that this be done not for my own ego aggrandizement but solely for the good of* (_____)." Our ego needs are subtle, and insidiously clever at hiding in our words. For co-creative commands to be powerfully effective, they must be made sincerely and powerfully from our heart and our gut, without hedging or choking. Co-creative commands that are in full alignment with the laws of the universe and the will of God manifest their outcomes instantaneously or at the right and perfect time.

ANGELS AS HEALERS

A major requirement of the mission and effort to reclaim this planet into light is that it must be done *co-creatively.* For that to occur, there must be a critical mass of human beings committed to the same goals—people whose intent is in alignment with the best interests of all people on the planet, now and into the infinite future. These must be individuals who have demonstrated consistency in their commitment, who have not wavered but who have kept their hearts and minds focused on the light, even while going through trying times.

This planet and all its people plus all our environmental, social, economic, political, and moral problems could theoretically be healed in a matter of nanoseconds, simply by the expressed will-command of God or the spiritual administrators of this planet. However, that is neither the best prescription for healing our woes nor the most productive way to bring us and future generations into cosmic citizenship. It simply does not provide for the much-needed soul growth that can only be achieved through the slow, evolutionary process of growing into the light.

Co-creatively reclaiming this planet into light will produce two profound outcomes. First, it will allow celestial beings to teach individuals how to bring their planet, nations, communities, and families into a new era of light and life. Second, on the human side, it will instill a sense of ownership in relation to the process, goals, and outcomes during this eon of evolution toward light.

The reason angels are so readily available for healing is that the more healed and complete humans become, the more spiritually, mentally, emotionally, and physically capable they become to co-create with the angels. *The next evolutionary developments in human activity depend upon the co-creative participation of mortals with angels.* Co-creative healing techniques are needed to provide leaders whose intent, sincerity, beliefs, and ego structure are in alignment with these developments. In other words, human civilization has just about reached the limits of its own inherent capabilities. Without extra-mortal participation, it is my view that human civilization cannot progress much more than it has. Retrieving the planet from this crisis will require the emergence of tens of millions of individuals who have healed their emotional issues enough to bring the next stage of a moral, spirit-infused civilization into existence.

Co-creative healing techniques are needed because twentieth-century society, communities, and families have become so dysfunctional that few families are able to produce spiritually, mentally, and emotionally healthy and well-balanced children who can eventually become the leaders this new era needs. Unassisted by spiritual influences, families cannot do this, public and private schools cannot do this, and churches or temples can no longer do this.

The bottom line is this: If the co-creative era had not been initiated earlier in this century, this world would be lost to increasing darkness. We as a planet of societies, cultures, and nations no longer would have sufficient spiritual mass to evolve into a world of light unaided.

It is no wonder, then, that angels are so readily available for healing. They have been working constantly with receptive humans, providing them with spiritual, intellectual, and emotional insights that have brought these new healing techniques into existence. In many cases, mortals and angels have had conscious dialogue with each other, which increased the progress of their efforts. Alternative healing techniques are one result of that cooperation.

A wonderful aspect of this time on our planet is that it is an era of healing, though this may be barely evident to most. Outwardly, healing will come first, then the discovery by thousands and then millions of people that healing is actually occurring. When that happens, we can expect that relationships of all kinds will improve rapidly and radically.

Rapid and radical healing of national and planetary issues depends upon the conscious awareness by more and more people that genuine healing can occur with the new co-creative forms. Individuals who are truly healed will rise to the top of their fields of interest, not out of egoistic, competitive need but out of service and love for others. They will be recognized as leaders of a new era. Then healing will occur from the top down and from the bottom up simultaneously.

9

Learning to Love

Love is at the core of spiritual mastery. It is the most powerful qualitative element of the spiritual journey. More than just a quality, it provides the energy for the journey. As we learn to love more consistently, we progress faster. Soon, living the journey and being love(ing) become synonymous. Learning to be love(ing) is the ultimate healing practice.

BEING LOVE(ING): DEFINITION

What is being love(ing)? It is both *being love* and *being loving*.

Being love is not a verb-and-noun combination we are accustomed to. We are very familiar with "being loving." But we can also *be love,* the full expression and embodiment of love.

Being loving involves *doing* loving acts and behaviors, *feeling* the emotional environment in ourselves when we are being loving, and *thinking* loving thoughts. For example, we tend to think of quality time with our children as time when we are being loving with them.

Being love(ing) combines these two phrases without excluding either. A person who is being love(ing) is both the embodiment of love and the expression and demonstration of loving thoughts, feelings, and actions. A person who is being love(ing) radiates love. When you walk into her presence you can feel the magnificence of her being; it is filled to over-flowing with love, which spills over whoever is near.

Being love(ing) is a practiced art, a skill that becomes more devel-oped, natural, and consistent with practice. Living consciously in the moment, we can use our will to bend our thinking, change our beliefs, mold our feelings and emotions, and guide our actions to become more and more loving.

QUALITIES OF BEING LOVE(ING)

When we think about love, being loving, and being loved, what is it about this state of being that sends quivers through most of us? The apostle Paul said several things about love (1 Cor. 13:1–14). I will include only what Paul said love *is* rather than what he said love isn't or doesn't. "Love is patient and kind. . . . Love rejoices when truth wins out. . . . Love is loyal. . . . Love expects the best from others. . . . Love goes on forever . . . and would all things vanish three things will remain—faith, hope, and love—and the greatest of these is love. . . . Let love be your greatest aim."

Love is accepting ourselves and others where we are, as we are. That is, love is unconditional acceptance. Love is not judgmental, prejudiced, opinionated, critical, biased, arbitrary, or exclusive, but is accepting, un-conditional, and inclusive. We respond to acceptance by feeling worthy—worthy of being an equal, worthy of being loved—and our worth is measured in love.

Love is appreciating ourselves and others where we are, as we are. We appreciate each other as God appreciates each of us equally. No one on our planet is of more value to God than anyone else. Some of us are just beginners, but that doesn't mean we are loved less than someone who has journeyed down the spiritual path for decades.

Our response to being appreciated is to recognize that we are deserv-ing. When someone says, "You are deserving of being appreciated," we should also appreciate ourselves for the best that others acknowledge in us. It is important to be appreciated by others, and it is equally important that we appreciate ourselves as others do, knowing that we are truly deserving of that appreciation.

DISCERNMENT WITHIN LOVE

While love is accepting, unconditional, and inclusive, it is also discerning. It is not that we love anyone more or less, but that we appreciate (weigh the development of potential in) each person differently. Love is universal, but respect, appreciation, admiration, and gratitude are individual. For example, a preschool teacher may love all of the twelve children in her care, but she appreciates each child differently—for the potential that they have learned to express in their being at that time. She loves and appreciates them where and as they are.

How do we learn to become loving and discerning at the same time?

First, we accept ourselves, emotional issues and all, without condition or bias—inclusive of all our being, without exceptions. That doesn't mean we always want to be as we are, where we are. It only means that we accept this point in our progress and we develop ourselves from there. We are neither critical about being at this point nor satisfied to remain here. It is just a given point in our journey, no more, no less. It's a bit like the slogan from the sixties: "No matter where you find yourself, there you are!" For those on the spiritual path, this statement becomes, "Well, here I am—what's next?"

Second, we accept others, issues and all, where they are, as they are. That doesn't mean we would like them always to remain where they are, exactly as they are, but that we want them to move on as they can, when they are able. Being discerning, we do not jump in and advise others how or where to proceed in their growth. Being discerning means letting others develop at the pace they set for themselves. If we intervene and try to help them carry their baggage on the spiritual journey, we may end up owning their baggage! Or they may end up carrying ours. We do not know why, where, or how people are on their spiritual journey. But if they ask for assistance, we can help without doing the journeying for them. We are always at our best when we neither intrude into others' spiritual journeys nor allow others to intrude into ours.

BASIC TOOLS FOR BECOMING LOVE(ING)

The basic tools for becoming healing—consciousness, will, and living consciously in the moment—are also the basic tools for (love)ing. Learning to be love(ing) is the ultimate healing practice that will replace all erroneous beliefs. *Willing* to love builds new sets of beliefs about ourselves and others by replacing judgment, prejudice, and exclusion with unconditional acceptance and inclusion. Learning to love and to be loving must become our core practice as we clear and heal our emotional issues and fill in the gaps in our mind where erroneous beliefs used to be.

ESTIMATING OUR PROGRESS

As we live more consciously in each moment, we can estimate the progress of our healing. As we become more and more loving, we will find that we also become less judgmental about ourselves and others. We make fewer decisions about how we and others ought to be and ought to do.

To assess our progress, it is necessary to know where we have been and what our goal is, and then to figure out where we are along the way. What truly indicates progress is our ability to love, accept, and appreciate others unconditionally.

Think back to chapter 6, "Overcoming Erroneous Beliefs." At the center of our unloving nature is a collection of erroneous beliefs that distort our thinking, words, and actions. What we will want to measure is the degree of change of our beliefs, but this is nearly impossible because our beliefs are not directly observable. However, we can do so indirectly by entering consciously in the moment and listening to our mind-talk. By comparing it to the mind-talk we used to have, and measuring both in relation to our goal, we can estimate our progress. The same goes for our "mind-videos."

Both mind-talk and mind-videos are direct reflections of the beliefs that operate on the conscious and subconscious levels of our mind. An *increased consistency* between our mind-talk/mind-videos and our intention to become more loving is an indicator of progress. By examining our mind-talk on the conscious level and our mind-videos on the subconscious level, we can see if there is agreement between our emotions and our actions.

We can also estimate our progress toward becoming love(ing) by examining what state of existence (*doing, being,* and *I AM*) we live in most of the time. As we have seen, our progress as a loving person moves through the earlier developmental stages of doing loving acts and being loving in our emotional state. Finally, we arrive at the place in our development where we are more and more loving in the I AM state of being. Fortunately, this state is not as distant as you may believe; each of us who yearns to have love in our life already lives at times in the I AM Love(ing) state of being. It may be only seconds, but that's a beginning. If we can be love(ing) even with a kitten or puppy, that's a start that can be expanded.

LOVE AND OUR EMOTIONAL ISSUES

If there is a clear dividing line in our emotional life, it is between our negative emotional issues and our positive loving qualities. This line is so distinct that it wonderfully reveals the work we need to do and the progress we have already made.

On one side of the line is the ego-self, which causes separation and isolation when it is out of balance. When living consciously in the moment on this side of the line, ask these questions: "What were my motive and intent for what I did, said, and thought? Are my position and my actions intended to aggrandize myself, and expand my ego at the expense of others? What do my actions say about my ego needs?" Whether we make derogatory comments about another person or conceited or arrogant statements about ourselves, the result is the same—separation on all levels from the other person. The unbalanced ego sees itself as exclusive of others and uses this exclusiveness to justify and rationalize its separation.

Any actions, words, or thoughts that create separation from others are almost universally egoistic in motive, intent, and result. Such actions are not being love(ing), no matter what the justification and rationale.

On the other side of the line is the magnificent, humble, loving, balanced ego. The loving ego actually erases the line between ego and others. The loving ego sees itself as inclusive, not exclusive; other people are not on the other side of the line—we are on the same side with them. Here, neither denying nor denigrating others, *we intentionally share this common ground for our own spiritual growth and to aid the growth of the other person.* This is the beginning of understanding what a sacred relationship is all about. It is the "we and us" side of the line. The spiritual path is not "us against them" or "me against you," or "me first, and I'll get to the Eternal Now before you do!" The spiritual path is a shared journey of sacred relationships where each of us aids others to achieve our individual spiritual goals.

When we make the effort to live consciously in the moment, and use these techniques for examining our behavior, we can quickly determine what we did to be love(ing) as opposed to what we did to merely stroke or protect our ego.

GOALS AND MODELS FOR BEING LOVE(ING)

Let us begin by clearly stating our goals for being love(ing). Although the goals we write down may seem overwhelming and almost impossible to achieve in this lifetime, they give us a direction in which to point our efforts.

The model for being love(ing) is the state of consciousness of spiritual Masters who met the challenge of mortal life and became Masters of it. Master Consciousness is in full alignment with God—the Creator, the source of all love—and a Master's relationship to God is intimate, personal, and continuous. The Master Consciousness lives as God-in-the-moment within the confines of a mortal life.

The secret of attaining this goal and model is to live life just one day at a time, one moment at a time. All the control we have over ourselves and our environment exists only in this moment, right now. The present moment is the starting line to begin achieving any goal, particularly the goal of becoming the full embodiment of being love(ing). That is, we strive to achieve being love(ing) by living just one moment at a time, and then extend that moment to include minutes, hours, days, and then the rest of our life.

There are several techniques for achieving the Master Consciousness in the moment. Which Master do you wish to emulate? For some it may be a Christian apostle; for others a saint or a prophet from the Old Testament; for yet others it may be an ascended Master, such as Gautama Siddhartha (Buddha), Jesus Christ, Confucius, Lao-Tse, Zoroaster, Mohammed, Krishna, the Dalai Lama, Mother Mary, or one of the Eastern avatars who is or was a practicing Master of being love(ing), such as Mother Meera, José Luis, Gangaji, Sai Baba, or Paramahansa Yogananda.

TECHNIQUES OF MASTERFUL LOVE(ING)

Technique 1

For a moment, a minute, an hour, or all day, take on as your alter ego the being of your spiritual model. Integrate into your life the qualities demonstrated by this loving being so he or she guides your decisions, your words, and your actions. Practice putting on the "cloak" of this loving consciousness; view the world and all its people, including both friends and antagonists, through the eyes of the Master. Feel the peace, calm, acceptance, and expansive thoughts this consciousness gives you. It embodies the total living acceptance of all that is. This is a relaxed state of being. It is always in the moment, at peace, and being love(ing).

Technique 2

Eliminate a *non-*Masterful aspect of your behavior, such as being judgmental, overly opinionated, protecting or embellishing your ego, or punishing other egos. Begin to examine what bothers you about yourself and release it. Don't participate in the games your mind starts. Your will controls your mind, so consciously steer your mind where you want it to go.

Technique 3

Do Master-Conscious activities and avoid situations that do not reflect that consciousness. This may be as simple as not participating in the personality bashing that often goes on during lunch hours and free time. If you can, just walk away from it. Staying and listening to negativity and emotional battering also has a battering effect upon us.

Technique 4

Review a recent emotional situation in which you could have been more loving. If you had been expressing Christ consciousness in that moment, what would you have done, said, or thought differently?

The goal of all these techniques is to live and express being love(ing) just one moment at a time. Being love(ing) is a force, a goal, and a process on the spiritual path. It is a process for healing our wounds and emotional issues, and is in itself both the evidence and the salve for further healing. It is a powerful antidote for the emotional hazards of human life on a tumultuous planet. When we practice often, we can become powerful living forces of light for the good of all who come into our life.

The importance of being love(ing) cannot be overestimated, for our emotional energy is the energy of our spiritual being. If our emotional energy is dark, our spiritual being will be dark. If our emotional energy is bright and effervescent, our spiritual being will be light and buoyant. Demonstrating positive emotional energy by being love(ing) can heal the greatest wounds in ourselves, in others, and on our planet.

While it takes courage to face our emotional issues, and greater resolve to heal them, it takes patience and persistence to become love(ing). It seems that the more difficult tasks involved in being love(ing) occur early in our spiritual journey when we are least prepared to heal ourselves and to be loving toward ourselves and others. With so few role models for being love(ing), our challenge is even greater, for each of us must reinvent the art of loving ourselves to heal ourselves. Surely when we become successful at this challenge, we will be mighty and strong souls.

Part III
Creating Sacred Relationships

10

Making It Safe:
The Ethics of
Functional Relationships

This chapter was originally designed for workplace settings, but it also describes the fundamentals for any functional relationship. The use of the ethical rules discussed here will help any relationship become functional, productive, and even enjoyable.

Almost everyone wants to be in a safe and open relationship, whether that is a marriage, a partner relationship, a work-team relationship, or a subordinate-supervisor relationship. Following ethical guidelines or rules provides a definitive way to achieve those ends, but it also requires the participation of everyone who is a partner in the relationship. Unfortunately, many people all too often play by their own rules. In a marriage, that will lead to antagonism and conflict; in a workplace, that will lead to grievances and worker-supervisor alienation, and the alienation of the line worker from the goals of the organization.

This chapter will examine the necessary ingredients for creating a safe relationship environment.

PREREQUISITES TO MAKING IT SAFE

The question below may seem rhetorical, but it is not. It is to be answered by each individual. It is important because it forms the foundation for a commitment to all that follows. Participants in the process of forming safe and productive relationships must first make a commitment that those goals are their own personal goals.

Do you want to create work, home, family, and community environments that are safe for relationships?

Yes? Then continue.

The paragraphs below provide an examination of what it takes to create a relationship safe enough that the participants can open up and be intimate, authentic, and trusting of one another. I use the word "create" as opposed to "make" because *creating in a relationship is a developmental process that requires cooperation*. Locks and gates can make safe surroundings, but only people can create safe relationships. It is not possible to make a relationship safe without participants wanting it to be safe. Two people who trust each other have gone through a process of discovering that they are safe to be authentic with each other in their relationship.

ELEMENTS OF A SAFE RELATIONSHIP ENVIRONMENT

To lay a firm foundation for building trust, creating a safe relationship environment is a must. There are several minimal qualifications to support and maintain a safe relationship, whether at work or in a sacred relationship at home. Each of these qualifications helps build consistency and congruence so each individual feels safe in the relationship. These qualifications work for both the receiver and the giver because each person in the relationship is always both.

"Keep My Communications Confidential"

I need to know that whatever is shared doesn't go beyond our conversation unless we agree that it is all right to do so.

"Accept Me"

Don't reject me because of my issues, emotional state, appearance, or physical proximity. We must feel accepted in our totality in order to be willing to risk, trust, and feel safe to participate fully in a relationship. This means acceptance of our beliefs, our emotions, our verbal participation, even our physical proximity, unless we agree otherwise.

"Stay with Me"

Don't pull away from me when I share my truth. This means that when we become genuine, open, and authentic in sharing our emotions, thoughts, beliefs, and expectations, you won't pull away from me. If you do, this tells me that you do not fully accept me, and that our relationship is conditional and tentative. This injures my belief, my faith, and especially my trust that our relationship is a safe one in which I can be emotionally authentic and open with you again.

"Support Me"

Offer me your caring, patient listening (don't jump immediately into presenting options for action) and your balanced emotional presence; provide genuine emotional support such as honest sympathy, caring, empathy, and statements that convey those qualities; offer me a thoughtful appraisal of the overall situation (of the events that caused the problem, my feelings, and the status of the current situation). Then offer me options for reasonable outcomes, if these do not add to my emotional burden.

"Honor Me"

All of the previous elements are included in my boundaries for being in a safe relationship. I need to know that you respect my emotional, physical, and relationship boundaries. When you observe them, you honor me. When we both honor these boundaries, we have created a safe environment where our functional or sacred relationship can be established.

Functional relationships of all types honor these rules in one form or another. I believe that participants in a relationship should come to a shared understanding of rules such as these for their own relationship, so that it provides all the benefits of effective relating.

ELEMENTS OF AN UNSAFE RELATIONSHIP ENVIRONMENT

It is as useful to understand how unsafe relationships occur as it is to understand how safe relationships occur. *Unsafe relationships occur simply because we let them.* Without thinking, we often give silent permission for our partner to believe that unsafe relationship conditions can exist and be tolerated. Safe relationships are created only through joint collaboration, but they can be destroyed quickly by acquiescence on the part of either member of the relationship.

An unsafe relationship exhibits the opposite behaviors of a safe relationship. Where there was confidentiality, there is inappropriate disclosure of personal matters; where there was acceptance, there is rejection or indifference; and so on. The result is the dishonoring of the other and an inability to achieve integrity, wholeness, and unity in the relationship.

BEHAVIORS THAT DISHONOR A RELATIONSHIP

If we think of a relationship as an interaction between a speaker and a listener, these are the kinds of behaviors that can comprise an unsafe relationship:

- Using shared issues against your partner (immediately or later) as attack or punishment.
- Violating your partner's physical space when he or she is feeling open and vulnerable.
- Distorting the magnitude or content of the issues of your partner.
- Telling your partner there is something wrong with him or her for doing, feeling, or being the way he or she is.
- Bringing up past issues or future consequences that magnify the emotional volatility of the situation for your partner.

- Jumping in before your partner is finished.
- "Dumping" your own load of emotional issues onto your partner before addressing their issues.
- Offering comments and suggestions for action before your partner is ready to hear them.
- Trying to fix or heal your partner without an invitation.
- Offering superficial or feigned emotions such as pity, patronization, or condescension.
- Minimizing or trivializing your partner's feelings or situation.
- Turning the situation into a "pity party" or one-upmanship game where you become the one with the problem, and your partner is shut out of the sharing.
- Projecting your issues onto your partner.

All of these behaviors cause separation between the listener and the speaker and are evidence that the safe relationship has become unsafe.

BALANCING INTRUSIVENESS AND DISTANCE

"It's none of my business" is probably the hardest thing to say to ourselves when we see our partner struggle with his beliefs, interpretations, and emotional reactions, whether in relationships with other people or with himself, or simply struggling to keep a positive balance in his checkbook. Helping our partner struggle with his problems by *not* interfering is difficult, especially when we believe that we know the answers before our partner does. The best course of action is to let our partner struggle to find the answers first by himself, before we interject our thoughts. This requires a delicate balance between being too intrusive and too distant. In all cases, we must honor our partner in his growth.

I often find that I must say to myself "It's none of my business" when I see my wife struggle with her challenges. Many times I catch myself taking a breath, preparing to tell her what I think she should do. As the breath rises from my chest into my throat to form the words, I remember that it is none of my business *unless her business intersects with my business.*

Before making suggestions, I remind myself to examine what she is talking about to determine if what she is struggling with involves me or any aspect of my personal business. If it doesn't, I don't say anything. If it does, I offer a gentle, straightforward question, such as "Is this an 'us' problem, honey?" or "How am I involved in what you are dealing with?" to determine whether I can best help by getting involved or by staying out of her business.

I have found that it is not helpful to pontificate, make bold statements of opinion, or use any phrases that include "you should" or "you ought to." When I do that, I become overly involved in her struggle.

Figuring out what is my business and what is her business is essential. It is the heart of discernment. It must be used to maintain the integrity of her identity, my identity, and our unique, shared relationship. If I intervene in her problems, issues, and other relationships as though they were my business, then we are on the road to becoming enmeshed, which makes a "mush" of our relationship. All of this leads to the following key insight:

Connectedness (without violating boundaries) and individuality (without creating isolation) are the essential parameters that distinguish functional from dysfunctional relationships, and safe from unsafe relationships.

MAKE IT SAFE: THE ETHICS OF FUNCTIONAL AND SACRED RELATIONSHIPS

It follows that these are the two basic ethical principles of all relationships:

- Connectedness without violating boundaries.
- Separateness without creating isolation.

These principles mean that even though two people are particularly close, they each have their own life, emotions, thoughts, beliefs, interpretations, and history that is unique and relevant to their life to share as they wish. These ethical principles provide the metaphorical landing lights that guide our relationship between the dangers on each side of the runway that leads to relationship happiness. For functional and sacred relationships, the extremes are enmeshment and isolation.

People who have not yet fully matured in their emotions find these principles very difficult to understand. The interaction of children with parents provides a visible example of the struggle to balance these two principles. From about age two until they have left home to live on their own, children are always trying to be separate but connected. Parents who are not emotionally mature often violate the boundaries of their children in order to remain connected with them or, at the other extreme, be separate and isolated. Tragically, emotionally immature parents and their children never achieve healthy interdependence. For travelers on the spiritual path, an imbalance between the two principles impedes spiritual progress and must be resolved to allow for personal spiritual evolution.

A functional/sacred relationship in which the two primary ethical principles are in harmony is a graceful duet, a dance between two partners who are in conscious emotional contact with each other, who yearn to share the other's emotional state without intruding or being too detached. In time, the duet becomes easier to perform without violating the two principles. The dance of these principles promotes the development of trust, confidence, greater rapport, support, acceptance, and honor for the partners. Our individual uniqueness offers an opportunity for admiration and appreciation rather than isolation and separation. Our commonality offers an opportunity for cooperation and integration rather than dependence and enmeshment. We come to trust that I will be me and you will be you, and that we will always be us.

COPING WITH CHANGES IN RELATIONSHIP SAFETY

Conditions in relationships always change; relationships often transition in and out of safe and unsafe conditions. But partners who are committed to their relationship make allowances for change and use it as a means to help each other grow in their emotional and spiritual character.

The safety of a relationship usually changes without mutual agreement as the result of a spontaneous need by one of the parties. If we preclude the possibility that people's needs can change, we limit how we participate in mature relationships or enter into new situations with old friends. We may even shut ourselves off permanently from friends who have become "unsafe" in their behaviors.

Abraham Lincoln said, "The best way to destroy your enemies is to make friends of them." When we are open to the possibility that people who have become unsafe to be with can again become safe, we may be able to save an old friendship. When existing friends become hostile, it is often best to be patient with them and, rather than make judgments, wait for them to ask for acceptance and inclusion into a safe environment once again.

RELATIONSHIP MAINTENANCE: EXPRESSING APPRECIATION

It is important to reinforce in others behaviors that are constructive and supportive, and that help maintain and enhance a safe relationship. Safe relationships are not to be taken for granted. *They are created through effort and maintained by more effort.* Expressing appreciation for creative, supportive relationship partners always strengthens the bond in a safe relationship.

Expressions of appreciation are evidence of sincerity and provide intimacy through the expression of our trust in the other.

Appreciation also includes the willingness to continue to appraise whether a relationship is safe or unsafe. For example: "John, you and I have become quite close in the last year. We have told each other about many personal situations, and have always honored each other's feelings and space. But recently in the lunchroom I overheard someone talking about some of the things I told you in confidence. Could you tell me what is going on? I need to know if I am safe in our relationship to continue sharing my thoughts and feelings with you."

Sometimes it takes courage to ask questions such as this, but the rewards for doing so always outweigh the negative consequences. Even when we lose a relationship partner by confronting him or her with questions regarding trustworthiness, we benefit by maintaining our own integrity and the integrity of our other relationships.

If we have done our homework and applied our training in maintaining safety to all of our relationships, the quality of our work life and home life will increase tremendously, or we will know very clearly what needs to be repaired. We will also discover whether we need to move on. Further, we will enjoy more authentic interactions with people we connect with even briefly, such as store clerks and others who serve us, or those whom we serve. We will gain a greater confidence in relating to all kinds of people, everywhere.

11

Building Sacred Trust

Trust is fundamental to co-creating productive, positive, constructive, functional relationships, and is the sacred ground of enduring partnerships. It is obviously critical to know who to trust and who not to trust, and how to discern the difference. This ability to discern can be developed consciously and deliberately.

Trust is one of the earliest social-relationship ingredients that develops in infants, and is central to the emotional and social well-being of people of all ages. The development of trust in functional and sacred relationships moves the participants away from the innocent, naive trust of infants to sacred trust that exists through conscious awareness in a mature relationship.

TRUST EQUALS BEING SAFE

Let us not mistake what trust is. Trust is the assurance that we are safe. When our safety is threatened, we should not trust. When we consider our degree of safety, we are actually evaluating our situation in the moment; when we trust, we extend the evaluation of our safety into the future. The following story illustrates the differences and similarities between safety and trust.

You are hiking along an old trail and come upon an impassable chasm. The precipice is sharp and there is no way down. So you continue walking until you come upon a footbridge made of rope and old boards. Is it safe to use? You know it has some strength because it spans the chasm. With a belay rope tied to your waist, you begin to crawl gingerly out onto the bridge. About six feet out you realize you are safe. However, though you are safe at this particular spot, you do not know if the rest of the bridge is safe. You continue farther, keeping your belay rope tight. Soon you are all the way across and on solid ground again. Looking back at your precarious trip across the bridge, you realize that you were safe all the way across. You now trust the bridge. Now you know you can cross it again and that you will be safe at any point along its span.

The evaluation of physical safety takes only a moment or two, but when we make an evaluation of whether or not to trust a person, that process takes significantly more time and experience. It takes time to weigh, deliberate, and discern before we can form an opinion or judgment about whether to trust or not to trust. Assessing trustworthiness becomes an extended process of determining how safe we are in this moment, the next moment, and as many more moments, days, or weeks as are necessary to know, really know, we can trust that we will be safe. But many people confuse immediate safety with generalized trust.

When you begin to weigh whether to trust or not to trust, think first of your safety. Ask these questions: Am I safe? Is this a safe situation? Will this be a safe situation when I return to it? If you can answer yes to these questions, then you can begin to correctly evaluate whether to trust or not to trust.

PRIMAL TRUST AND DISTRUST

The need to develop trust is deeply ingrained in our physical, social, and emotional makeup. Try for a moment to conceive of trust from the point of view of a wolf in the wilderness. For a wolf, trust is not a social/behavioral concept but a matter of conditioning. Wolves learn to trust from learning what other wolves in the pack do. As pups, wolves learn that they will be cared for, nursed, fed, cleaned and groomed, weaned, taught to go on excursions; they will then hunt, mate, and so on. Their life course is predictable. Even the behavior of the dominant male of the pack can be counted on. It is not a matter of deciding whether to trust or not; only that which is "wolfness" is trusted within the pack. Wolves from outside the pack who travel through or join the pack are kept at a distance and observed until their "wolfness" becomes known. The new wolf is either in alignment with the pack, in which case it is safe and can stay, or it is excluded from the pack.

For human infants, it is much the same, provided the parents are trustworthy. If the mother and father are trustworthy and dependable, the child will learn trust as the wolf pup does.

What this tells us is that trusting and not trusting emanate from the deepest strata of our mind, particularly our subconscious mind, where ingrained beliefs get locked into place as a result of experiences with adult caregivers. Primal attitudes of trust or distrust are formed when we are infants; they become determining factors of our behavior that originated as beliefs about the world based on what humans "in our pack" actually do.

DISTRUST AS A KEY RESULT OF UPBRINGING

Why would someone deliberately and willfully act on the basis of relationship values that produce inferior and dysfunctional relationships? I believe the answer involves the need of individuals to be in separation from others, which is undoubtedly a learned factor in their upbringing. We see the results all around us: All too many people live in separation from others even while living with them, or are emotionally isolated from friends and associates because in their childhood they were ingrained with the belief that other people are untrustworthy. When this belief is lived out, other people become objects to be manipulated and used—or avoided.

Having worked in prisons for many years, I have heard dozens of authentically spoken statements that tell volumes about how the prisoners felt about themselves, their lives, and their relationships. Their opinions about other people provided clear evidence that they had been consistently treated as objects and used by others. Time after time I heard statements such as "I'm just looking out for number one." "Me first!" "I've gotta get mine first or I'll never get it." "You just can't trust anyone." "People have always dumped on me. Why should I care to have friends?" "Why should I have kids? A wife? Are you kidding?" "People are for using. Use them first before they use you." "Kids are just sick people who haven't grown up yet." And many more.

Our American culture is pervaded by attitudes like these, particularly characteristic of the "Me Generation" of the seventies and eighties and heard nearly as often in ordinary society as in prisons. Unfortunately, we will probably witness much more of this from the children who grow up in the homes of "me first" parents.

Again, the central reason for such untrustworthiness is inferior upbringing. For example, people who are untrustworthy have learned from their dysfunctional caregivers that inconsistent verbal statements (fibs, prevarications, untruthful statements, half-truths, misleading statements, and outright lies) produce relationships with inferior qualities (dysfunctional relationships), or that such behavior may lead to the termination of a relationship.

It is understandable that training and practice of functional relationship values may be missing from a person's background. There is hope, though, that this sad situation of dysfunctional beliefs, expectations, and relationship skills can be healed, and that the individual's life can become personally, socially, and spiritually functional and prosperous.

Indeed, it is possible to build trust where none existed before. The premise of that hope is the very concept of a sacred relationship: two individuals who have, to a great degree, worked through their own issues and are dedicated to being trustworthy within themselves and with their partner.

I'll admit that it's an impossible challenge for some. During my experience working in prisons, I met several earnest men who wanted to know how to make it on the outside. I told them that they needed to be honest with "regular people," to be consistent in what they told them, to be open, and to respect the other person. Their response was almost always the same: "The truth? Ya mean the 'truth' or the 'real truth and the whole truth, so help me God?' Well, man, that's crazy. If I do that, I'll get ripped off. If I don't pad my time card at my job, for instance, 'the man' will short me my time. So I figure if I pad my time card, and he shorts me, then I come out even and so does he. Isn't that fair?"

I found that truth and trust are not fairy tales but horror stories and science-fiction thrillers to those who were not raised with truth or trust in their lives—except for the "trust" and "truth" they concocted to serve their own ends.

THE BASIC ELEMENTS OF TRUST

In our relationships with others, certain attributes inspire us to trust. I have found that dependability, consistency, and honesty are the cornerstones of trustworthiness.

Dependability

Our dependability should be evident in our actions from moment to moment, month to month, and year to year. If I am dependable, then when we agree to meet at Alissio's Espresso Bar at 10:15 AM, I will be there at 10:15. It's often as simple as that!

Consistency

We are consistent when our words match our actions and what we espouse is congruent with how we live. Consistency is vital to our own well-being and our relationships in at least three ways.

Perhaps the most immediate way is its effect on our body's sense of emotional balance. Let's say, for example, that your mother or close friend asks, "How are you and your partner doing with the new baby in your life?" You say, "Fine, we're doing just fine. We're not having any problems at all." Actually, though, you feel miserable because of postpartum blues and the new financial burden of being away from work, as well as from lack of sleep. And to be honest, you're generally feeling miserable about your life since you came home from the hospital. In this situation you can expect to feel a knot of energy in your solar plexus: Your body is noting the inconsistency between your words and feelings.

Second, any mismatch between our emotional state and what we say gets imprinted in our auric field (personal universe energy field), where others can sense its presence. They will intuitively sense an inconsistency between what we say and how we feel. Sacred relationship partners are particularly sensitive to this imbalance of energy and should mirror what they notice back to their partner.

Third, the lack of congruence between our real emotional state and what we say can have an immense impact on our children, causing them to experience emotional confusion—or worse. It can jeopardize the development of any functional or sacred relationship.

Honesty

To be honest is to tell the truth all the time, and in doing so to provide complete information—conditioned by wisdom.

Being completely honest is a praiseworthy quality in itself, but it is not always wise or practical to be totally honest in certain situations. Consider the necessity of guarding very young children from information they are not mature enough to understand when they ask straightforward questions about where their sister or brother came from. On the other hand, if my mate is concerned that I've been drinking too much and asks how much I am drinking every day, do I hedge my information? No. In this case, guarding the information would be merely a defense for my inadequate ego and would cause undue separation between myself and my mate.

So the question of honesty can be a sticky one. As a general rule, withholding information to protect our ego must be avoided, but revealing too much information such that it causes injury and distance from the other person is also to be avoided. In all cases, we need to be very honest with ourselves to determine who is being protected and why.

Aside from these, there are other building blocks of a trusting relationship, such as respect and openness. These also have roots in our ability to trust: When we trust, we *respect* our own thoughts, words, and feelings, as well as those of our listeners. When we are authentically and personally receptive to another person, we are being *open*.

STEPS IN BUILDING TRUST

Mature trust is built over time upon hard evidence of trustworthy behaviors; it is not an instantaneous process. The development of trust is just that, a developmental process that goes through several stages:

Stage 1: The Gathering of Evidence

This part of the process is investigatory. In collecting evidence, we are nonjudgmental and at the same time intentional. Nonjudgmental listening is an excellent way to begin: Hear the other person's words and how she uses them—these are the most direct evidence of what she believes and how she interprets situations.

In doing this preliminary information gathering, we learn about the person's trustworthiness long before we take additional emotional risks to discover their deeper secrets. Undirected chitchat and polite conversation are a waste of time if we want to discover whether our trust will be well invested. If instead we carefully choose questions to ask, we can un-cover the bases for their opinions, interpretations, and beliefs, as well as their particular life history that led to the formation of these core ideas.

Our observations and the person's past performance are the best in-dicators of the level of congruence we can expect between what they say and what they do in relationships. Although they may lie, distort, and provide half-truths, as a careful listener and observer we can discern the difference.

Stage 2: Acceptance of the Person Socially and Emotionally

At this stage of developing trust, we gauge the feelings we have when we are in the person's proximity. The first test is mere acceptance of being in their physical proximity: If we feel physically unsafe in their presence, we have no business being in a romantic, financial, or other close relation-ship with them.

Probably one of the most assuring signs that we can accept someone is our feeling of emotional trust—it feels good in our belly and heart to be with them. When we trust someone, we feel at ease with her, and we accept her emotionally without reservation or hesitation. Trust is never complete if we have lingering reservations about the other person.

Stage 3: Forming an Opinion on the Potential of Trust

Next we develop an opinion within ourselves whether to trust the other person, although the opinion may be tentative and noncommittal. Some-times this stage is brief in the development of trust; for example, I might say to myself, "I can't find anything untrustworthy about him. I think he may be trustworthy."

Stage 4: Making an Admission or Commitment of Trust

This stage also is brief. After continued observation and interaction, you say, "I have decided he can be trusted. I now make a commitment to trust this person as a reliable friend or partner."

Stage 5: Operating with Trust as a Given in the Relationship

This stage is developmental and ongoing. From the point of admission of trust, the commitment and trust deepen. In time, it would take a great deal of evidence to overturn this commitment of trust. Ironically, at a certain point, it will take more evidence of untrustworthy behavior to *overturn* the commitment of trust than it took to *develop* that trust in the early part of the relationship.

THE BELIEF IN REASONABLE TRUST

Our belief in a mature, reasoned trust must be developed slowly. Building the belief of reasoned trust in another person can be done only by living consciously in the moment. In addition, being intentionally conscious of building trust will add strength to the trust-building process. One must keep in mind throughout that there are no shortcuts to building mature, reasonable trust.

The following example illustrates trust-building as a process that grows slowly between a man and a woman who will eventually become committed partners in an intimate relationship.

Two people travel on the same electric commuter train for several years. They observe each other but never meet, not because they aren't attracted to each other but because there is no strong impulse to do so. Both have been married, but eventually divorced and are now single.

He notices that she always arrives at the train platform on time, is neat and well dressed, and has a confident but not commanding presence. She is always polite to others and does not push her way into the train car, but waits to find a place to sit that suits her. She is not a compulsive worker, but reads novels, the newspaper, and women's magazines, and does some work without imposing a strict routine on herself.

She notices that he regularly rides the same car as the one she chooses. He is always well dressed, neat, and wears clothing that is "soft" rather than hard and commanding. His ties are floral or other designs in warm colors. She notices, too, that his face is nearly always composed and has a gentle appeal. He sometimes catches her eye, but does not make an issue of it or approach her. He seems at peace.

Both of our characters are on the same train car the morning it stops in mid-commute. The conductor announces that a truck has toppled one of the supports for the overhead electrical wires and the train will be stuck for several hours before the damage can be repaired.

They are sitting in tandem on opposite sides of the aisle. As if on cue, they simultaneously turn their gaze toward each other with looks that seem to say, "Oh well, worse things could happen."

"Hi, my name is James, James Canby," he says evenly. "Looks like we get to enjoy either an anxious, tension-filled few hours or a leisurely commute to work. How do you view it?"

"Good morning. Just call me Jul," she offers. "My name is really Julia, but that sounds a bit old-fashioned to me. To answer your question, I think we are going to have a leisurely ride into the city."

"I'm glad to get to know you, Jul. I've taken this train, and usually this same car, for several years and have seen you here too, but never had the right opportunity to introduce myself." He gestures to the empty seat beside her and asks, "Do you mind?"

"No, not at all, please do," she replies, and smiles as she pats the empty seat beside her.

This brief exchange and the history leading up to it contain significant bits of interpersonal information relating to the development of trust. The particular ways this couple phrases their statements, plus their nonverbal behavior, were key indicators of the appropriate level of trust.

First, each had observed the other over the years and had come to know a fair amount about the other, and had already come to trust the behavior of the other person as dependable and consistent. Though the rings on their fingers had come and gone, the turmoil of the events that brought that about did not shatter their lives or spill over onto other people on the train in uncomfortable ways.

Second, they had intuitively felt a similarity between them that they could not explain. Their observations had included all the regulars on the train, but neither of them had developed the same comfortableness and ease as they felt for each other. It was as though they knew this but had remained reserved about it. This led them to believe that the other was socially and emotionally safe even though they had never spoken. Now it only remained for them to experience the process of getting to know each other to validate the opinions they had formed.

Do you see from this example how trust is reasonably developed?

First there is *observation,* gathering evidence without being in overt contact with the other person. These observations include hundreds of minutiae that we usually do not think about. For Jul these included the texture of the clothing James regularly wore. It included the designs on his ties, the care he gave his hair and how he styled it, and the composure of his face, which she had noticed in hundreds of micro-observations.

James noticed the subtle fragrances Jul wore from time to time, the length of her skirts, the style of her shoes, the cut and style of her hair, and the care she gave her hands and nails. He, too, had a large composite library of micro-observations of her gestures, facial expressions, and postures, from which he interpreted that it was safe for him to approach her and introduce himself the day the train stood still.

The opinion that each had formed about the other was based on thousands of observations and hundreds of interpretations, but with no firm beliefs or experiences of trust or distrust. Were they being too cautious? I don't think so. Each had come to know through experiences in childhood, adolescence, and adulthood that truly good and enduring relationships are based on predictable, consistent behavior. Each, as a divorced person, had come to know that the potential of an intimate relationship cannot be developed hurriedly; it takes far more time to create a committed partnership based on the belief of full trust than it does, for example, to form a work relationship at the office.

Why is the subject of trust so important? It is because few of us take the time to be like "civilized wolves" that observe, observe, observe, and observe some more before we trust. As for distrust, many people do not give a violation of trust the full weight of significance they should to avoid further pain and disappointment in a relationship.

The best course of action we can take is to develop trust very slowly. Developing trust slowly is wise because the investment of trust often needs to support a partnership for a long time and the investment of a person's life in a relationship may become deep and total. The closer and more intimate the relationship, the slower we should go, because when we finally say to ourselves, "I trust this person," we open the way for all else that follows. This is another way of saying that we need to make the process of developing trust intentional and conscious.

UNWARRANTED BELIEFS ABOUT DISTRUST

If there is even a hint of distrust, our next step in the experiential process of developing trust must be to examine whether our observations and opinions of another's trustworthiness are accurate or in error. Is the other person really untrustworthy, or is it our beliefs about relationships that are faulty? If the person is truly untrustworthy, then we ought not to enter further into that relationship; but if the person is trustworthy and our faulty beliefs are the culprits, then we must replace them with functional ones. Otherwise we will prematurely eliminate potential friends and loved ones from our lives.

It takes courage—courage of Herculean dimensions—to enter into this intense examination of our personal beliefs about relationships. I have known many, many people who have foregone the possibility of friendship and love in order to avoid the uncomfortable examination of what they really believe. They would rather be alone than examine their own beliefs about relationships.

So what do we want—unprejudicial, reasoned acceptance of others and the potential of unlimited friendship and love, or the unexamined, comfortable acceptance of our own beliefs about others, even when the latter can only deliver evenings alone in front of our forty-eight-inch television screen night after night? What does this result say to others? It says that we are untrustworthy in relationships. People who sense that will limit our involvement in their lives, and rightfully so.

REMOVING OUR PREJUDICIAL BELIEFS ABOUT TRUST

What are such prejudicial beliefs? Aren't they *beliefs based on unfounded distrust* of another? This kind of distrust, whether it goes by the name of prejudice, denial, exclusion, lies, bias, deceit, judgment, bigotry, or arrogance, does not serve us on our spiritual journey. Removing prejudicial beliefs is probably the most difficult thing we can do. No one else can remove them for us. Only we, individually, can do that.

I have discovered that most people who have prejudicial views know and acknowledge that their opinions about others are prejudicial. If your beliefs are prejudicial, you can remove them just as you would other erroneous beliefs: (1) know there is an alternative; (2) decide to remove them; (3) act on the decision to remove them.

Step 3 may involve asking a person we are prejudiced toward to enter into dialogue with us. If we are unable to do this directly, we can ask someone to facilitate the dialogue or act in behalf of the person. This process may include admitting we feel nonaccepting toward someone.

We could say, "I need your assistance to help remove my prejudices. They seem to be getting in the way of developing a potential friendship with you. Would you help me?"

If the person says yes, we can ask her to tell us about herself, then *listen,* and listen carefully. This will allow us to get to know that person and her beliefs, hopes, desires, fears, and joys. This simple approach will help us see that person outside of our colored beliefs and prejudicial views.

(There are, of course, real scoundrels in this world who cannot be trusted. It is the object of this training to help you *discern* potential friends from potential scoundrels.)

The process I have been describing is a real, functional example of what socially healthy people do many times a week, either directly or indirectly, to develop new friendships. It can also be used over and over again to maintain existing relationships, be they old or new.

We must make a commitment to listen to others so we can overcome fixed ideas about them; sometimes it can literally be a matter of life or death. For example, parents who have lost a child to suicide almost always express deep regrets that they were not courageous enough to listen carefully to their child to discern his or her state of being long before the painful event occurred. Though it can be difficult, embarrassing, and frightening to ask probing questions, we must do so literally to preserve our relationships. I have known divorced people who wished they had listened carefully to their errant spouse and asked probing, discerning questions long before the thought of divorce had surfaced.

In new relationships, the process of being authentic and finding trust often works best when the threat of emotional turmoil is imminent. When the vagaries of a relationship journey has taken the "ship of our relation" to the point of breakup, trying to sail in calm seas and sunny skies may seem impossible. If you are in a relationship that is in storm-tossed seas of emotion, continue to go to "relationship night school." Try to learn new skills and practice them in a safe environment before you pull in the sails, tie down the tiller, and batten the hatches all at once. You didn't get to this point of distress in your relationship journey overnight, so it may take a while to get back to a safe harbor. At least you can learn enough to keep "your side of the ship" away from the rocks of destruction.

DISCERNING TRUSTWORTHINESS

As adults, we need to sort out issues of trust quickly so we can live life more easily and consistently. "Trust no one" is as unproductive as "Trust everyone." Neither rule will serve us well; neither position will provide productive, functional relationships. But do we live in a society where we can assume that we can enter into relationships with trust? What provides the best possibility for building safe, healthy, and productive relationships—entering with trust or with distrust?

Perhaps the best position is the middle ground, as we saw with the earlier example of Jul and James: to enter a relationship tentatively, being watchful for signs of untrustworthy behavior, without investing too much of ourselves in the relationship. Whether the new relationship is simply paying the gas station cashier or meeting a person we would like to see often, each opening provides ways of developing trust while using caution.

It is far more productive in the long run to enter into new relationships cautiously, building trust as time and association with that person progresses. If we trust implicitly and discover that we were taken advantage of, reentering that relationship to build authentic trust is much more difficult.

On the other hand, distrusting everyone in every relationship situation but keeping a wary eye out for trustworthy behavior will not be productive either. That is because the underlying belief in this case is *distrust*. Such beliefs are a self-fulfilling prophecy: Any evidence that seems to support that belief "proves" that the belief of distrust was justified to begin with.

In the end, people who are intrinsically distrustful will never find trustworthy friends. That is because most people are still in the process of becoming perfect, so they exhibit a certain amount of "slippage," or discrepancy between what they say and what they do. In addition, we know from our experience that circumstances change and the timing of life sometimes requires us to change plans before we can inform others.

Those on the infinite path of spiritual evolution also have times of discrepancy. Sacred relationship partners willingly and lovingly confront each other with these discrepancies so they can work on their issues together. In doing so, we do not abandon or threaten our relationship, and our partner is not threatened by our gentle, loving confrontation. She accepts confrontation as one of the dynamic aspects of our sacred relationship. We provide a nonjudgmental mirror to our partner so she can learn, and she will do the same for us.

Whether we are in a committed partnership or a passing relationship with a cashier, discerning trustworthiness is a fine art. *A mistake many of us make in assessing trustworthiness in others is to take sincerity as evidence of trustworthiness.* I can honestly say that some of the most sincere individuals I ever met were in prison.

Let us not be naive about trust. A person who says, "Stick 'em up! I'm going to take all your money and valuables" sincerely intends to do just that. His behavior is predictable and consistent, and you can trust that he will proceed to rob you. Your evaluation of the robber may be, "Yup, he's a good robber, all right. He did what he said he'd do." But that obviously does not mean you should maintain an ongoing relationship with the robber. Yet many of us continue relationships with people we know are sincere but *whose intentions violate the relationship.*

Many times people continue to participate in their own victimization because they are attached to the sincerity and earnestness of their assailants. I have seen this pattern over and over again in misguided parents who have such a relationship with their criminal children.

Any evidence of the misuse of a relationship for personal advantage is an indicator that you should withdraw from that relationship. Examine the intentions of the person in whom you are placing your trust. Are her intentions worthy of your trust? Is she deserving of your trust? Are you safe with that person?

Life gets a lot easier when we learn to discern quickly whom to be in relationship with. Why equivocate? Keep life simple—enter into and maintain only those relationships that are safe and trustworthy. Once you have discerned which relationships are probably safe, then proceed to consciously and intentionally build more trust and make the relationship safer.

DETERMINING YOUR BOUNDARIES OF TRUST

It is essential for us to know our boundaries of trust and distrust, to know what makes a relationship unsafe for us. Some of us have boundaries that are so distinct that any violation of the trust/distrust boundary makes continuation in a relationship unsafe. It is helpful to review our boundaries for trust and distrust with a thoroughly trustworthy friend. Talking them over with a friend allows us to question, examine, and weigh the critical elements of our trust/distrust boundaries. It is important for us to challenge our criteria for safe and unsafe boundaries to discover if they are reasonable or unreasonable.

In overhearing older women talk about their relationships with men, I have heard such statements as: "Never trust a man who wears bib overalls." "Never trust a man who keeps his own checking account." "Never trust a man who goes to movies by himself." And many more. Are these boundaries reasonable? What are your boundaries of trust for people's words, actions, and emotions? If you don't know, develop them. To assist you in being more conscious of your trust/distrust boundaries, here are some important questions to consider:

How do we recognize trust? Isn't it evident in honesty, consistency, dependability, loyalty, dedication, devotion, faithfulness, truthfulness, and discretion?

How do we identify trust in the realm of emotions? Isn't it evident as unconditional love, caring, compassion, appreciation, acceptance, and related supportive and socially nurturing behaviors, words, and thoughts?

How do we know who to begin to trust? This becomes evident when we observe another who is cooperative, consistent, and an effective team player who coordinates, consults, and listens. Does this person use discernment and know how to make right choices and decisions, displaying qualities such as patience, forbearance, and even sacrifice when needed? What level of intimacy, authenticity, vulnerability, and childlike acceptance does this person demonstrate? Has he established boundaries for himself and others? Does this person know about taking/giving, giving/receiving, receiving/sharing, sharing/letting go when it comes to conversations, discussions, opinions, objects, gifts, and services?

Should we trust in what people say? Are the statements of the person worthy of trust? Does the person make statements condoning or supporting antisocial, unethical, or immoral behavior? Are the statements of the person meant to manipulate others in any way? Are all her statements true? Are there ever any discrepancies, untruths, half-truths, or lies? If so, take more time to build trust.

Should we trust in what people do? Are the actions of the person honorable? Does the person engage in antisocial, unethical, and immoral actions? Is there consistency between what she says she will do and what she actually does? Does the person take action without first disclosing her intention to take action?

Should we trust in the other's emotions? Are the person's emotional reactions appropriate to the situation? Does he try to manipulate the emotional reactions of others? Does he use his emotional reactions to manipulate others?

Any evidence or behaviors that would or have produced harm or abuse to others is cause to distrust that person. People get hurt when they trust unwisely, when they believe they are safe when evidence indicates otherwise, or when they trust when there is not enough evidence to indicate trust.

THE ENERGY OF TRUST AND DISTRUST

The energy of trust and distrust is palpable in close personal and intimate relationships. If one person has violated the relationship in some way, the other person can feel that violation. However, what most often occurs is that the person who feels the energy of distrust often denies what he is feeling.

Those who appreciate the comfort and security of trust find that distrust feels prickly and uncomfortable. Spouses and partners experience it as similar to the feeling generated by unfaithfulness. You might not know for a fact that the other person has violated the relationship, but the feeling of distrust is there.

What you do with what you feel is obviously up to you. When to talk about your feelings of distrust will probably depend upon how long the relationship has existed and whether there is any outward evidence to support your intuitive feelings. Patience and caution should be used depending on your assessment of how risky the situation is.

MAINTENANCE OF A TRUSTING RELATIONSHIP

Many people know more about how to maintain their cars than they know about building and maintaining relationships. A relationship does not have any moving parts and does not require changing oil, rotating tires, or replacing brake pads, but maintaining one is far more intimidating for most people than taking care of the car they drive. And it is often thoughtlessly ignored. Yet we are in relationships all the time, sometimes long after they are no longer operating, or even after one of the "passengers" dies. Our relationships offer the greatest and most rewarding potential for our own fulfillment if we know how to operate and maintain them well.

Maintaining a successful relationship involves the same processes as discovering, developing, and placing trust in another person.

1. Spend time with your partner; discover more about the other person.
2. Listen to the other person and be emotionally present and available.
3. Accept him as he is, where he is in life.
4. Appreciate her for participating in the relationship.
5. Give him an opening to invest his time and energy in the partnership.

6. Become self-revealing.
7. Tell him and show him how much you trust him and what you are doing to maintain your relationship. This last step is not done self-gratuitously but to make the other person aware of what you are doing and why.

Functional and sacred relationships cannot exist without trust, the bedrock upon which earnest people build long-term, enduring, loving partnerships. Building trust in any partnership is a *learned relationship skill.* Critical in this process is *discernment,* learning how to determine who to trust and who not to trust. This process can make life seem treacherous, because for most people this learning is done one person at a time, one mistake at a time. Yet it does not have to be threatening. As we have seen, there are proven and safe ways to discern who to trust and who not to trust. The wisdom that comes with age, the written word, intuition, and intentional and conscious efforts to discover trust will save us from a lot of relationship anguish.

12

Understanding Pain and Disappointment in Relationships

It may seem odd that this chapter appears so late in this manual since, unfortunately, most people focus on the misery in their relationship before trying to discover and heal its underlying problems. *Pain, anguish, and disappointment are only symptoms of problems in a relationship.* When we are living consciously in each moment, the appearance of pain and disappointment should act like a ship's horn in the fog, warning us to ask, "Why is this unhappiness, pain, and disappointment in my life?"

HAPPINESS IN RELATIONSHIPS

Why do pain and disappointment occur in relationships? In my view, understanding how and why partners are *happy* in their relationship is the best place to begin. Playing detective, let's track down why happiness occurs by asking some provocative questions.

Isn't happiness an opinion or estimation of the condition of the relationship according to one or both of the partners? When someone asks, "How's your new relationship going?" the response may be "Really well. I enjoy it." That is the partner's estimation of the condition of the relationship at that moment.

Next detective question: "How did you come to the estimation that you are happy in your relationship? How did you arrive at that opinion?"

The response might go something like this: "Oh, I just think this is the way a happy relationship should be."

Next question: "What led you to think that?"

"Well, it's what I *believe* a happy relationship should be."

Our rejoinder becomes "Oh, so your happy relationship is what you have *expected* a happy relationship to be like. Is that right?"

"Yes, certainly. Thank you—you said it better than I did."

In this little dialogue we have come quickly to the core of the reason for happiness in a relationship: The current state of the relationship matches the expectations and beliefs of both partners for that relationship. *The better the match for both partners, the greater the degree of shared happiness.*

UNHAPPINESS IN RELATIONSHIPS

We can logically deduce from this that unhappiness is a result of unfulfilled expectations. *Disappointment is simply the recognition that our expectations have not been fulfilled.* Disappointment is what we feel when our expectations, either agreed upon or assumed silently, are not realized.

Our expectations develop from our beliefs about relationships, and from our experience of what actually occurs. *If we do not share joint beliefs and expectations about the relationship, we will always be disappointed.* Disappointment may be followed by unhappiness, pain, disillusionment, distancing, and alienation, and even acts of overt betrayal, unless the mismatched beliefs and expectations are consciously and intentionally exposed, examined, and brought into alignment to become shared beliefs and expectations.

Relationships with matched beliefs and expectations develop in the same way as those with mismatched beliefs and expectations, only with opposite outcomes. This is as valid for labor contracts and unwritten agreements of friendship as it is for marriage contracts.

WHO IS RESPONSIBLE FOR HAPPINESS IN RELATIONSHIPS?

Your next question must be "Whose beliefs and expectations get fulfilled when I am happy?" Your answer: "*Mine,* which means that I am responsible for my happiness in relationships. That includes *all* relationships, whether my marriage, a business partnership, my relationship with the car repair service manager (and even my car!), my neighbor, my employer, my children, my parents—everyone."

In what I call a shared relationship, the answer to the question "Whose beliefs and expectations get fulfilled when I am happy?" is "*Ours.*" That's because the beliefs and expectations are explicitly shared. You can see that being a responsible partner in a shared relationship is a serious matter. Each partner is responsible for 100 percent of their own happiness and 50 percent of the collective happiness in the shared relationship. In effect, each partner is responsible for 75 percent of all the happiness in the relationship.

That sounds ominous and weighty—no one to blame for our unhappiness, disappointment, and disillusionment! Perhaps you were raised by a co-dependent parent who might also have been alcoholic, or maybe you lived with a rageaholic partner or a rebellious teenager, or had a mean and grumpy neighbor or landlord, or perhaps a demeaning and demanding supervisor or manager. In all these cases, you might think that attributing happiness and unhappiness solely to yourself is just so much garbage. You would be partially right. While we are ultimately responsible for our own happiness and unhappiness, the cause of our unhappiness is often other people—initially. Though our partner might come home drunk and curse us, how we react and how we handle our expectations, beliefs, and happiness in regard to the relationship is totally up to us.

STAYING PRESENT TO THE RELATIONSHIP

Take some time now to close your eyes and make conscious contact with your physical body, your emotional body, and your mind. Notice your degree of emotional balance, as well as your thoughts, mind-talk, and mind–video clips. Slowly review each meaningful relationship you now have: with yourself, your partner, supervisor, employer, neighbors, mother, father, children, and anyone else who is important to you.

What is the state or condition of your relationship with each of these people? Are you happy/fulfilled/frustrated/angry/dissatisfied? Are you unhappy about some part but not all of that relationship?

Ask yourself why you are unhappy with that relationship or a part of that relationship. Do you feel any emotional pain? Do you feel anything at all? If you're not happy but you don't feel any pain, then everything is all right in your relationship, right? Wrong!

If we are not feeling pain but are also not feeling joy, happiness, fulfillment, and contentment in a relationship, then we have skipped feeling the pain and moved into the never-never land of being numb and dumb in the relationship. (Never-never land: never feel and/or never admit you have any pain.) If we don't feel any pain, it is essential to go beyond the numbness and try to get in touch with it. Recognizing and feeling the pain is fundamental to understanding its causes. This must occur before it can be removed and its causes healed.

Pain, anguish, and disappointed feelings are only symptoms of the mismatch of expectations and beliefs between relationship partners. Covering up the symptoms by drinking or using drugs, partying, staying busy, shopping excessively, or engaging in some other kind of "-aholic" activity only masks the real reasons for the pain, anguish, and disappointment.

Let's say you tell a friend, "I've had this really sharp pain on the right side of my stomach just below my belt line. I think I may be wearing my belt too tight, causing my clothes to chafe the skin where the pain is. I bet if I just loosen my belt and wear softer clothes for a while, the pain will go away." You do so, but the pain doesn't go away, and the next day you're in the emergency room with a ruptured appendix. The point is that *treating symptoms (pain)—whether physical, psychological, emotional, social, or relationship—is unproductive in the long run.* Symptoms are only signals, much like traffic signs and lights that say, "Hey, stop and look! The problem is nearby. Take a closer look!" But so often we get caught up with merely treating the symptoms, which will never heal the causes of the pain.

Living consciously in the moment is the foundation for healing the causes of our unhappiness, pain, and disappointment. Living in the present moment, we can feel directly the pain of a relationship situation. We can say, "Ah, I feel pain. I am disappointed and I feel very unhappy." Our next response should be to ask ourselves and our partner, "Why? What is it about this situation that is painful and makes me feel unhappy?"

Living consciously in the moment means having the awareness to question whatever we are experiencing at the time. Question it; if no questions, no answers. Don't just accept the pain and continue suffering. Ask questions of it; search for reasons. Don't just stand there, feel something!

HEALING RELATIONSHIP UNHAPPINESS

As children, many people were erroneously taught that they were not complete in themselves. Many adults believe that when they get into a relationship, their "other half" will be added and they will be complete and whole. But the reverse is true: Because relationships magnify and multiply dysfunctional relationship skills, they may feel even less whole, as if the fractions of wholeness in each person must be multiplied instead of added. The result of multiplying one-half by one-half is one-fourth! The point is that if two miserable people come together in a relationship, the relationship will only magnify the misery of each partner. Partners must overcome their erroneous expectations and beliefs in order for their relationship to become satisfying and fulfilling.

Healing unhappiness in a relationship can begin when partners:

1. Live consciously enough in the moment to acknowledge that they are unhappy, their expectations have not been met, and there is a mismatch of beliefs and expectations about the relationship.
2. Dialogue to discover the expectations each has about the relationship.
3. Dialogue to discover the beliefs each has about the relationship.
4. Dialogue to discover the origins of their individual beliefs.

Be prepared for steps 1 through 4 to take a good deal of time. It may be helpful to have the assistance of a relationship facilitator or coach.

These beginning steps provide the partners with the opportunity to get in touch with not only their own beliefs and expectations and the origins of their beliefs but, just as important, the beliefs and expectations they generate together. Sharing this process may bring up a lot of childhood pain and anguish. When the partners are emotionally supportive, the process will deepen the emotional bond between them.

The first four steps can become a wonderful way to heal the immediate aspects of relationship unhappiness while that bond is being strengthened. After this has occurred, these next three steps will come into focus. The partners must:

5. Negotiate new, *shared* beliefs and expectations. This process may be extensive and may need to be reworked several times. Replacing old beliefs with new ones is like rewriting a "software program" in your mind. But unlike computer software, you will need to imprint the new beliefs and expectations many times before they will automatically become a part of your database of expectations. I write mine down on sticky notes and place them where I will see them often, then read them silently and aloud several times a day for several weeks.

6. Review the new beliefs and expectations after a reasonable period of time. Be prepared to make subsequent changes in your living habits. It may mean, for example, that *you* will take the dog out for exercise each morning rather than your partner. That means talking about it the night before to make the transference of responsibilities complete, resetting your alarm clock, and setting out your jogging suit that evening.

7. Participate in another review later to see how the new beliefs are working. If both partners' expectations are still not being met, perhaps some minor tinkering is necessary or the expectations need to be adjusted once again.

It is helpful to work through the steps objectively, with a minimum of egoism. By fully engaging in this step-by-step process and striving to live consciously in the moment, you and your partner can co-create a relationship that is functional and enduring. This process can be applied to business and work relationships as well.

Methods for dealing with severe emotional injury caused by the violation of the relationship by one of the members is the subject of chapter 7, "Getting to Forgiveness."

PERSISTENT UNHAPPINESS IN A RELATIONSHIP

Persistent unhappiness in a relationship could indicate a greater problem than a mismatch of beliefs and expectations. It is usually a symptom of one or both partners not being emotionally mature and responsible, or even socially functional. Most of us have not had the benefit of being raised in a healthy family setting, with functional, mature, responsible, and loving parents. We arrive in adulthood with incomplete socialization and dysfunctional relationship skills along with erroneous beliefs. Or we were left to form our own conclusions about life without having guidance from a wise and reliable adult or authority figure.

Even these conditions have a remedy, *if* the person with these difficulties is willing to admit his or her deficiency and can consciously live in the moment. As we have seen, when situations arise that cause unhappiness or social discomfort, one must be aware enough to ask "Has this situation come to me because I have some inner work to do related to it?"

Being able to ask such a question takes a lot of self-awareness. It also takes a great deal of humility to ask ourselves if we are the real source of our difficult relationship situations. We must make a sincere search through the inventory of our expectations and beliefs, the indoctrination of our childhood, and the whole array of our adult learning experiences to find the underlying causes.

FUNDAMENTAL GUIDELINES FOR FUNCTIONAL RELATIONSHIPS

I have found seven fundamental guidelines that support happy, satisfying, and fulfilling relationships. They are presented here neither in priority order nor in the order of developmental process.

Fundamental principles of functional relationships:

1. Live consciously in the moment.
   a. The present moment is the only place to fully appreciate the pain and disappointment you are experiencing and give them their true value.
   b. This moment is the only time to resolve pain and disappointment.
   c. The present is your only opportunity to fully appreciate the happiness you are experiencing and share it.
2. Expect the unexpected.
   a. The beliefs about yourself and your partner for the relationship will change.
   b. Anticipate that your expectations and your partner's expectations for the relationship will change.

3. Relationships are an adventure. It is wise to go on an adventure prepared for the best and worst weather.
4. Relationships do not end, they only change in outward form.
5. Relationships are processes, not objectives.
6. Your partner is not perfect; neither are you. You will each make mistakes.
7. Love, acceptance, appreciation, trust, forgiveness, and mutual respect can heal any mistake in a relationship.

As we have seen, pain and disappointment in relationships are directly caused by a mismatch of expectations and beliefs by one or both partners. Sometimes the pain is shared and sometimes it is not. Pain and disappointment, being only symptoms of deeper underlying problems, offer the opportunity for exploration into the unknown territories of the relationship. Indeed, pain and disappointment occur because undisclosed aspects of a relationship have not been examined or resolved.

Because relationships do not end but only change form, pain and disappointment continue to offer the opportunity for both partners to jointly explore and deepen the emotional bonds between them so that the relationship becomes stronger and more enduring. Recurrence of painful and disappointing relationship situations need never arise when partners live consciously in the moment and accept pain as an opportunity to venture into those unknown territories.

Yes, it takes courage to adventure into the unknown and, yes, it takes humility to admit deficiencies in ourselves that may have initiated the unhappiness. Yes, it takes love, patience, forbearance, kindness, and compassion to wade through the muck of each other's life and our own life to arrive together at a shared understanding of the renewed relationship.

Functional relationships are the frontier of adventure and development for conscious explorers in the late twentieth century and into the twenty-first century. Now is the time to discover ways of sharing your life that are personally fulfilling, happy, and satisfying, with a partner who is experiencing life the same way.

13

Discovering and Living with Your Ideal Partner

This lesson incorporates many elements from prior lessons, reframed in terms of sacred relationships. Finding our ideal—or what I call right and perfect—partner takes in all parameters of the previous chapters. A conscious and intentional, functional and sacred relationship embraces the totality of this awareness and the skills taught in this manual.

The title of this lesson may seem to point to an impossible goal, but that goal can be reached. It is much like the placement of the last massive stone block on top of Cheops pyramid: A lot of work and the accomplishment of many small goals had to occur before it was possible. Finding your right and perfect partner is in many ways like putting a capstone on your spiritual journey.

"CONSCIOUS" AND "INTENTIONAL" DEFINED

"Conscious" is used throughout this book to mean "aware." To be conscious of self is to be aware of self. As we saw in chapter 3, consciousness of self means that we are aware of being aware of ourselves—what we do, what we say, and what we think. "Intentional" has been used throughout to mean "premeditated" and "deliberate"; these synonyms indicate the practice of thinking before taking action.

The qualities of consciousness and intentionality must be cultivated in order to bring a functional or sacred relationship into existence. The *conscious* aspect of the relationship requires that we live with awareness in each moment of our partnership, particularly when we are in each other's company. This doesn't mean that we need to walk on eggshells when we're with our partner, as that would be a sign that we have become co-dependent. But we do need to be aware of the impact of our behavior on the one we love. For example, we communicate thoughtfully and with sincere intention, never using sarcasm or other word games. Partnership is difficult enough without throwing mean words around.

The relationship is also *intentional* in that it is a premeditated and deliberate relationship that exists to support each partner's personal, emotional, and spiritual goals and the goals of the relationship. Couple practices can be intentionally initiated to create clear outcomes and results.

FUNCTIONAL RELATIONSHIPS DEFINED

A functional intimate relationship is one in which all actions and processes in the relationship are constructive and positive, and contribute to the individual goals and the shared goals of the participants. Each partner becomes the mirror for the other's emotional baggage without participating in the other's emotional dramas. Doing so provides each partner with a safe emotional space to more quickly work through unresolved emotional issues and to develop the emotional and social potential that lies within.

Why do we need a mirror for our emotional baggage? Because when we are in the midst of an emotional event, we are usually unable to objectively examine why we reacted as we did. That requires someone who is objective and not a part of the emotional event, someone we trust and know will help us, not hurt us or add their own baggage onto our load when we are upset.

My partner is at her best when she reflects my emotional dramas for me like a high-quality mirror. That occurs when she provides a clear image of me without distortion, by being detached from what is happening to me and within me, and by helping me think through the emotional event that I experienced. As functional partners, we facilitate our partner's emotional growth by acting as an unbiased mirror, reflecting an undistorted view of our partner. Acting as a mirror is not an excuse to mock or mimic our partner; likewise, when our partner mirrors our emotions back to us, we must not attack her for doing so.

Effective mirroring will not occur if we try to force the healing process that our partner needs to go through. As the neutral mirror, we simply help our partner live consciously in the moment to examine her beliefs and expectations as they exist now, rather than remaining stuck in the past or in the future.

Mirroring for our partner involves two key activities: listening carefully and reporting and sharing our insights. Listening is relatively easy, but reporting and sharing our insights must be done with tact and love, which requires great consciousness.

Our insights into our partner's growth quite often apply to us as well. With loving, spirit-filled partners, the insights for one often become the insights for growth of the other. As one or the other partner moves ahead, this progress can provide a straighter path and more advanced insights for the other's growth. As a result, individual and mutual growth is spurred on and is often rapid.

SACRED RELATIONSHIPS DEFINED

A sacred relationship has all the qualities of any functional relationship, with the added feature that when we act as a mirror to our partner, we do so to aid their spiritual development as well as their psychological growth. This means that in sharing our insights for emotional growth, we question our partner and ourselves: "How would the Master have handled this situation? How would he have reacted to this situation? What would he have said to you about it? More important, what does God-within-you suggest you do or say?"

When we explore these questions, we act from our own higher consciousness to draw our partner to the threshold of the spiritual "Aha!" that would occur if a living Master were working directly with our partner. If we are able to do this in a nonreactive, nonintrusive, emotionally detached way, we can be a catalyst for our partner to transmute their emotional energy into psychological insights and spiritual awakening.

AN ILLUSTRATION OF THE SACRED RELATIONSHIP PROCESS

The following story may help you understand some of the dynamics of this kind of effective mirroring.

A young couple had gotten married with the conscious intention of living in a sacred relationship. Everything was going along fine for them until the new bride, Jil, began having problems at work. For several days, she came home after work tearful and depressed. Her husband, Ben, became concerned about this new development in their life and decided to practice being Jil's emotional mirror. He waited for a day when she would come home feeling particularly upset by her work.

One late Friday evening, after the bank had closed and Jil had balanced out, she arrived home after an especially difficult day. One of her co-workers, Erroll, had been mischievous and taunting. He was very competitive and bragged to Jil every day about all the extra services he had gotten customers to sign up for. He repeatedly told Jil that he was the one, not she, who was going to win the bank's prize of a trip to Hawaii.

Jil kicked off her snow boots, let her coat fall on top of them, and threw herself into the nearest chair. She sobbed silently, her shoulders quaking with the release of her pain. Though her tormented state was almost inaudible, Ben, who had been in the study, knew his wife was having quite a time of it, and walked quietly into the living room where his wife was sitting.

In a low voice he said, "Sweetheart, you're upset. Do you want to talk about it?"

"Ben, work isn't fun anymore. I'm not happy."

After a pause, Ben began to probe further into his wife's work situation. "Why isn't it fun anymore?"

"Oh, that damned Erroll!" she exploded. "He treats me just like my little brother did when we were growing up. He's always bragging about his accomplishments and tells everyone he's going to earn more points than me for the trip to Hawaii. I don't even care if he wins or if anyone else wins. I just don't like being belittled by him in front of all the other employees and customers."

A glimmer of understanding crossed Ben's mind and a slight smile came to his lips when he realized that he could help his wife with her problem. "So tell me, sweetheart, what was the one thing your little brother did that made you so angry with him?"

"Oh, Ben, it happened so long ago it doesn't seem worth repeating."

"No, seriously, tell me about it. You said that Erroll reminded you of your little brother. Maybe there is more to this than you think."

Wiping her eyes and taking a deep breath, Jil began to explain how her little brother John had always competed with her. She related that he had become very mean, and when eventually his accomplishments were not enough to displace his sister's, he began to talk about some of Jil's personal habits and behaviors with adult friends of their parents when they came to visit. His treatment caused her great humiliation and embarrassment, so much so that she eventually became very withdrawn when visitors came to their home.

Gently, Ben continued, "Did you ever reconcile your hostility with John?"

"No. No, I never did. I didn't have a chance to. John became a Marine and was killed in Somalia. I feel really ashamed that I am still angry at him. I love him and I even forgave him for what he did to me, but I am still angry at him. Ben, I feel ashamed for still being angry with him even though he's gone."

"Oh, you needn't feel ashamed. Your anger is very real, and you still have a reason for feeling that way." Ben continued, "Now, think for a moment of the times when you were angry with John. You felt angry at him for the way he treated you, but how did you feel about yourself? He made you angry, but what were your feelings toward yourself?"

"I felt powerless, and stupid, and . . ." She took a deep breath and exhaled. "I was the older child, but I felt belittled. I felt like a little kid who had wet her pants at the movie theater and everyone knew it. He exposed all my weaknesses in front of everyone. I wouldn't stoop to his behavior to get back at him. It was just too absurd and incredibly mean."

"Jil, it sounds as though you have forgiven John, but have you forgiven yourself for feeling bitterly angry with him, particularly now that he is dead?"

"No. I never thought of it that way. I forgave him but I didn't forgive myself."

"Do you see any connection between what he did to you and how you felt about yourself then, and what Erroll is doing to you and how you feel now?"

A long pause followed Ben's question. Jil slowly began to answer the question as flashes of insight came into her mind.

"So you mean that what Erroll is doing triggered my old memories and feelings from when John used to taunt and harass me?"

"Yes."

"Well," Jil continued with new excitement, "so I'm afraid I will look stupid in front of customers, my supervisor, and the managers. I guess I'm also afraid that there won't be any resolution to my situation. I feel as though it will go on and on. What do you think I ought to do?"

Ben could see that Jil was beginning to get the larger picture of her situation, and her excitement was catching. "Honey, if you have sincerely forgiven John, can you forgive yourself for feeling and acting depressed, unempowered, and embarrassed as a kid in front of everyone?"

"I think I can," she replied thoughtfully.

"Then go one step further and also forgive yourself for being angry with your dead brother. Say the words out loud that you forgive yourself. Close your eyes and see yourself in the form of the Master."

Jil closed her eyes and said with a smile, "Yes. I see myself in the Master's form, just like we have practiced before."

"Now, as the Master, speak to Jil, who is in front of you, and forgive her for having those harsh negative thoughts about herself. Can you do that, Jil?"

"Yes. As the Master, I see little Jil sitting on my knee and she is looking right at me."

Jil began to play the roles of both the Master and little Jil.

"I'll ask her, 'Jil, do you know how much I love you?'"

"Yes," replied Jil as her younger self, "I know that you love me as much as anyone, even the angels God made."

"Yes," continued Jil as the Master, "I love you as much as I love myself. And Jil, I forgive you for having such negative thoughts and feelings toward yourself and John, the ones you felt when John taunted you."

"Master," said little Jil, "I forgive myself too. I didn't know any better. I wish I'd had you as my friend then. I think I would feel a lot better about myself now if I had known you then."

"Now you can love yourself, all of yourself, little Jil. Can you love yourself as you were as a little girl? And can you love yourself and forgive yourself as big Jil?"

Now Jil was in the role of both the young Jil and herself. "Yes, Master, I do love myself as you love me, and I forgive myself, both as little Jil and now, today, as big Jil, the one who works in the bank."

Breaking from her role playing, with tears of gratefulness and joy streaming down her cheeks, she said to Ben, "Oh, Ben, it is so wonderful to make the connection between the Master and myself. We have it inside of ourselves all the time, don't we?"

"Yes, we do." Now Ben was beginning to choke up and his eyes were glistening with the emotion he felt for his wife, and with feeling the Master-connection that he had renewed while he was listening to Jil and her process.

"Do you think this process will help you with your situation at work, honey?"

"Yes. I know just what to do. I'll silently be the Master and help Erroll too. I know I can do it without belittling him or embarrassing him in front of anyone."

Feeling empowered from regaining the energy that she had locked away in her feelings as an anguished child, Jil asked her supervisor for an appointment and arranged for Erroll to be invited too. There she revealed her personal reactions to Erroll and her supervisor. Without accusing Erroll, Jil was able to help him understand how his behavior had affected her personal life, both on and off the job.

Erroll apologized for his behavior, which he explained as "just fun," and reassured Jil that he would keep his bragging to himself. The supervisor had provided a safe space for Jil to tell her story and empowered both Jil and Erroll to work together without infringing upon the ego of either one.

When people "push our buttons," as Erroll did to Jil, we often act like a tape recorder that keeps playing the old beliefs we have about ourselves, which we then act out and hurt ourselves with. But if we were grounded in the moment in the Master Consciousness, we would see through the playback episode and let it pass through our mind without getting caught up in our old tapes of shame and pain.

When we can live consciously in the moment with our partner, we can strive to become the Master of our consciousness. If we get lost in the drama of our emotional reactions, our sacred relationship partner can help us slow down the action in any situation so that we can carefully: (1) observe what is going on; (2) decide how we will interpret the situation; (3) decide how we will react; and (4) act in the Master Consciousness.

The conscious awareness that our partner is our ally in the processes of our sacred relationship is highly stimulating emotionally. In a healthy relationship, each partner provides feedback about what the other is feeling and helps them process those feelings in positive and constructive ways. The relationship then becomes dynamic and capable of transforming itself as the beliefs and expectations of the partners change. When this occurs, we have become conscious, co-creative partners in the relationship.

CO-CREATING YOUR RIGHT AND PERFECT SACRED RELATIONSHIP PARTNER

If you are not currently in a relationship or if the one you are in now is not satisfying and you have decided to bring that partnership to a close, this is a good time to consider how to co-create your right and perfect mate or partner.

It is a well-known metaphysical axiom that what you put into the universe comes back to you multiplied many times over. If you release love to the universe, you get back love; if you give forgiveness, you get back forgiveness; if you give resentment, you get back more resentment. So if you want to co-create your ideal mate and partner, it follows that you must first co-create that person within you. You must become the kind of partner you want to attract into your life.

One of the benefits of walking the spiritual path is that we become more and more balanced, centered, grounded, and healed. The emotionally wounded child gets healed, grows up, leaves home, and builds a life of his or her own, then seeks his or her right and perfect mate.

But there is a caveat to the "right and perfect" aspect of this lesson. Earlier we considered the wonderful truth that when we ask, our angels will help us progress along the spiritual path. By the same token, they will also help bring your right and perfect mate to you if you so request. However, if you do not specify *when* you want this perfect partner to show up, the angels will determine that for you as well.

Right now you might be thinking that if you were to declare "I want my right and perfect mate to show up now!" then the angels would cause your right and perfect partner to show up now. However, that person would only be the right and perfect mate for your spiritual development *at this time*. In other words, the person who shows up will assist your spiritual growth perfectly for the current phase of your journey.

Not to be outfoxed by this development, you might be saying, "Dear God, bring my right and perfect mate to me for the rest of my life." Having said this, you will need to wait until you are ready to be the right and perfect partner *for the rest of the other person's life too!* That may be immediately or it may take weeks, months, or years until you reach a stage in your emotional and spiritual evolution where you can sustain your half of that relationship.

"Aha!" you say, "I'll just ask for my right and perfect mate for the rest of my life to show up *now*"—which takes you right back to where you started. Certainly, if there is no conflict between "right and perfect," "for the rest of my life," and "now," then—voilà!—you can expect to meet this person soon. But if there is any conflict, then the angels and God will arrange it according to what is best for you. Remember, our unseen helpers have our best interests at heart. But they are not on a linear time schedule; their schedule is developmental, not temporal.

It may seem impossible to discover our right and perfect partner, but it really is not. One of the gifts of being on the spiritual path is that so much help is available; we are not alone in our efforts. By stepping onto this path, we have put ourselves in the flow of the universe. Instead of pushing against the river, we have chosen to flow with it. Rather than forcing ourselves to find our mate, we wait for our mate to be brought to us as we strive to improve our other relationships, including our relationship with ourselves!

If we consciously do as much as we can to rid ourselves of the emotional baggage we picked up in our childhood and adolescence, and ask

℮ ORIGIN PRESS

If you wish to be placed on our mailing list to receive notices about other books from Origin Press, please send us this card.

PLEASE PRINT

Name _____

Address _____

City _____ State ____

Zip or Postal Code _____

Country _____

Visit us online at www.originpress.com

◉ ORIGIN PRESS

1122 Grant Avenue, Suite C
Novato, California 94945-9809

God and all of His unseen helpers of love and light for assistance, we will have prepared the way for our partner to be attracted to us. You can be assured that if you have done these two things, your partner is already on his or her way to you.

14

Relationship Paradigms

Once upon a time, marriage partnerships were conceived of as naturally fixed and unchanging, assuring a lifetime of emotional security for the partners. Today, we know this to be a fairy tale of cruel proportions. Out of the death of this old paradigm of relationships has come a far healthier and more functional understanding: Union or partnership can create security and even permanence, but that permanence must allow for continued change and growth. It is truly possible for two people in an intimate partnership to remain together for many years, but they must be conscious of the "morphing," or changing, of their relationship. Further, they must intentionally design a relationship paradigm or set of paradigms they want their relationship to grow into, and then consciously guide the ongoing changes of their relationship in that direction.

The purpose of this chapter is to help you examine different paradigms of relationship so you can make more conscious choices about the kind of relationship you want and how you would like it to evolve. You can then work toward co-creating your partnership by learning the beliefs, expectations, values, and role interactions appropriate to the paradigms you have chosen. These then become part of your developing expertise for living in the partnership you have intentionally designed.

When you and your partner learn to manage the evolution of your relationship more consciously, you will be better able to flow and shift with the inevitable changes that come in any union. When we build a framework of beliefs for our intimate relationship that includes the unexpected, then such changes can be anticipated and planned for. It then becomes a part of a progressive evolution that can make the relationship a great adventure.

EXPLORING THE PARADIGMS

Relationships are rarely limited to one paradigm. Most partnerships exist as combinations of paradigms that evolve and devolve, and no particular evolution is typical of all relationships. Each relationship has its unique pathway.

As you read through this list, simple but tough questions will probably arise that can help you become more conscious of your relationship intent. For example: "Is my relationship to my partner primarily a social one? Have I chosen it because it can provide me with the social contacts that could make my career take off?" If you answer yes to these questions, but your partner has a different intention for your shared relationship, the two of you can expect to eventually encounter some big problems.

Take the opportunity this chapter provides to explore what you really want. Typically, if we have not looked at a potential partnership through the lens of the different paradigms, it is almost certain to fail. Hidden "relationship land mines" that are not discovered can cause major problems later on. That is why many relationships eventually "blow up."

The Single-Interest Paradigm

Many relationships exist to provide a specific, clearly definable means by which partners can share a mutual interest. These include physical, social, emotional, intellectual, and spiritual interests. However, this kind of relationship is narrow in its function and does not provide a wide base of common interests or interaction for maintaining a long-term relationship. For example, I know a couple who were athletes in college and decided to get married. Their center of activity was in the exterior world—their only common interest was athletics—but eventually they became parents, and taking care of the baby became the wife's new priority. She no longer had the time and interest to maintain the focus on athletics she had shared with her husband. Sadly, the couple quickly became distant from each other. But this kind of problem does not have to be permanent; if the couple can develop a new relationship model that allows for a wider scope of shared interests, they may have new hope for growing close again.

Though a relationship that is based solely on one narrow interest is obviously very limiting, some highly successful relationships begin in this way. The partners who do make it work are those who become conscious of the problem, and set an intention to explore other paradigms in their new relationship.

Goal Paradigms

The primary function of goal relationships is to accomplish a shared goal, which can be permanent or temporary. Goal-paradigm relationships provide a means of achieving security for the partners. The shared understanding is simple: By achieving the goal(s) of their relationship, the partners will become secure in what they value most. These partnerships can also provide means to measure growth of the self-worth, self-esteem, and social value of the two individuals. Couples in these paradigms can often point to an external goal and measure their progress toward fulfilling it, and even compare their progress with other couples who have similar relationship goals.

The *survival paradigm* operates when partners come together for the purpose of basic survival. Monthly adventure magazines often contain stories of life-or-death incidents that have drawn two people together. Their physical survival is dependent upon the effectiveness of their relationship—for example, a couple who have crashed in the wilderness in a small plane, two dogsled drivers who are trying to win a race across the Arctic, or two mountain climbers who are the sole survivors in their team after an avalanche. Though the survival paradigm is described here in terms of the untamed outdoors, sometimes partners live in an urban wilderness where survival is just as precarious and dependent upon the faithful functioning of each partner.

The *frontier-pioneer paradigm* is a familiar scenario in which partners come together for the purpose of challenging the "frontiers" of their lives. (These relationships can make for good movies, as in *Far and Away,* starring Tom Cruise and Nicole Kidman.) The frontier may be a major lifestyle change, such as moving to another country, recovering after a destructive tornado, or any other situation where the couple faces the task of reorganizing their individual and shared lives to overcome some external challenge. This paradigm is closely related to the survival model, and elements of both are often operating, depending on the severity of the challenge.

The *procreative paradigm* has as its major goal or function the birthing and raising of children. This paradigm has become somewhat less common in the late twentieth century as other paradigms have taken precedence in Western societies. (A large brood of children used to be a desired asset for couples who needed strong bodies to help work on the farm.) Some religions still encourage the procreative paradigm for theological or dogmatic reasons.

The *acquisitive paradigm* seems to have supplanted the procreative paradigm for many late-twentieth-century couples in the developed world. The goal of these "doing" couples is to acquire more and more property and financial assets. In the U.S., the trend is for urban couples to come together chiefly to acquire the "good things" of life, choosing not to have large families.

The *retirement paradigm* has as its goal the "easy life," which is a logical continuation of the acquisitive paradigm. Having saved and invested their income over the decades, the retirement-paradigm couple can begin to use it to settle in at home and do the things they enjoy but never had time for during their working years.

The *traditional American work-ethic paradigm* comprises a continuum of external goals that can include the survival, frontier-pioneer, procreative, acquisitive, and retirement paradigms. The goals of the partners in this type of relationship are to survive, fulfill the challenge of their shared life experience (frontier), produce a family with children who will provide grandchildren, acquire material and financial assets, and retire to enjoy grandchildren and ensure the eventual transference of their remaining assets to their children "so they do not have to work so hard" in their adult life.

Regardless of their benefits, goal relationships have inherent difficulties: The partners can become so invested in achieving their shared goal that they lose sight of the good functioning of their relationship independent of their external objective. After the goal is achieved, the partners' sense of purpose may begin to stagnate because they no longer have a role to fulfill.

In essence, goal relationships are externally driven; they subordinate each individual's emotional and spiritual growth to those areas of interest that support the shared goal. Making external achievement the highest priority tends to limit divergent evolutionary influences that are essential for individual and relationship growth. Ultimately, the goal becomes primary, and individual satisfaction and happiness become secondary. This result will become a source of distress and division in the relationship unless partners maintain a clear, ongoing mutual agreement that reaching the goal supersedes the other aspects of the partnership.

The Service Paradigm

It is not uncommon for two people to come together to be of service to the world in one way or another. Such couples serve together in many professions and areas of interest: Politics, religion, and education are some obvious examples. Based on what you learned about the goal paradigms, you can imagine that if the specialized service a couple is providing does not succeed, or if the success wanes, the relationship is in danger of collapse. A collapse of their joint mission will force the pair to reevaluate the purpose of their relationship. For a couple's reevaluation to be complete, they must examine the shared areas in the relationship that remain and truthfully answer these two questions: "Do we still have enough in common that we can continue our relationship in another paradigm?" and "Do the differences we brought to the relationship, which once were complementary—or at least did not interfere with our ability to serve together—now exist only as opposites?" As in any other paradigm, a conscious intent to incorporate new goals or shared interests can save the partnership, if that is desired.

Other Paradigms

Examples of other paradigms include the platonic, romantic, erotic, and recreational. These can operate alone or as part of a single-interest, goal, or service paradigm. Here are a few examples: "Mary and I had a strictly erotic relationship. Neither of us had further expectations, and we enjoyed it while it lasted." Or "Teddy and I have a recreational, romantic, social relationship. We play the tennis circuit, both enjoy being romantic, and socialize with our international friends. We plan to enjoy it as long as it lasts, though we don't have any intention to get married. We know how to do this pretty well, and we both agree that we don't think we could do the marriage thing successfully. Neither of us had good role models that set a good example for a successful marriage. So why try?"

These cases provide an important insight about every successful relationship paradigm: The partners know their capabilities and limitations and have consciously set boundaries and shared expectations for their relationship.

The Sacred Relationship Paradigm

Partners in a sacred relationship can have any of the goals and values characteristic of other paradigms, but the commitment to the spiritual growth of each partner is the primary focus.

To use a stage-play metaphor, we could say that two people in a sacred relationship are at once actors, directors, production managers, and the audience of their relationship. The sacred relationship process is a means for the actors to iron out their emotional issues so that the production of their play (relationship) can flow smoothly. Through the conscientious use of the sacred relationship paradigm, fewer and fewer emotional issues crop up, which allows the partners to devote more attention and effort to becoming spiritual partners. Just as in a stage play with new actors, once they have overcome their mutually detrimental emotional issues, they can concentrate on improving their acting performance and capability.

Love Alone Is Not a Paradigm

I believe that the two major reasons intimate relationships fail are: (1) the partners are not conscious of their relationship as an unfolding process that needs ongoing attention, and (2) the partners have not declared a conscious intention for actually being in their relationship. Unfortunately, love alone does not supply either of these vital ingredients.

I realize that it may be astounding to say that love alone is not a sufficient reason for a relationship to endure over the years. Love by itself simply is *not* a relationship paradigm; it is, however, a very necessary ingredient to help the relationship successfully function in the chosen paradigm. Love could be seen as the "hope chest" of the relationship, from which each partner draws to extend patience, forgiveness, understanding, sympathy, empathy, loyalty, and faithfulness. For a young couple to decide they will get married and remain together forever just because they love each other is not wise. I suggest that they decide on a series of relationship paradigms that will form the basis of a solid commitment and then consciously examine their relationship day to day and week to week, just as any conscientious business owner would do to ascertain the financial and overall health of the business.

PARADIGM SCRIPTS

Let's look closer at the metaphor that compares intimate relationships to theater plays. Every relationship (play) has partners (characters) who have roles in the play. Each character's role is defined by the *scripted beliefs, expectations, values, dialogue,* and *role interaction* of the characters.

The relationship paradigms described in this chapter also have such well-defined roles and role definitions. The roles you and your partner play in your chosen paradigm can be analyzed and scripted so that over time you develop a set of beliefs, expectations, values, role behaviors, dialogue, and interaction that support and guide your relationship.

Taking time with your partner to do this now could save you a lot of time talking across the desk of your accountants and attorneys later. It is important that partners develop supportive, caring, sharing, loving ways to interact. We all have seen the opposite—couples who play out the script of the "contest paradigm" of relationships. Here, each partner takes an adversarial position on any subject, accompanied by much shouting, berating, cursing, threats, and other detrimental behavior.

Why then are some relationships successful and others not? For the same reasons that some long-running Broadway plays are successful: The script is tight and has a universal appeal to the audience; all the actors know their lines and are thoroughly familiar with the lines of the other characters they interact with; and each actor fully understands the dynamic of the interplay of their character with the other characters.

Also like successful plays, successful relationships are not dependent upon props, sets, backdrops, or costumes. As most of us understand but rarely fully appreciate, lots of money and property do not make for functional long-term relationships.

For brevity, let us pick a simple relationship paradigm to show you how to discover your own paradigm script. I chose the romanticism paradigm as my example because in almost every culture and society, romantic behavior exists in one form or another, at one level of development or another, though some cultures are more inclined toward romantic behavior than others.

A CLOSER LOOK AT THE ROMANTIC PARADIGM

Romanticism means "love-play," with frequent interludes filled with tender words, caresses, kisses, hugs, and strokes, so that the partners feel physically accepted. Love-play also includes going out to socialize, being with other couples, showing your partner that he or she is socially accepted by you. Romantic love-play is a way of showing and assuring your partner that there are no physical, social, emotional, intellectual, or spiritual barriers between you.

Romanticism provides a veneer to a relationship that enlivens it without being detrimental to the partners' emotional and spiritual growth. For romanticism to be a successful part of the relationship, it is essential for both partners to smoothly play out the reciprocation of their roles, behaviors, and values. Let's discuss this paradigm in terms of these elements:

Roles: Giver and receiver; each partner is the giver and receiver in every giver-receiver episode.

Beliefs: Unexpected giving and receiving demonstrates an outward show of inner love for the other person; special episodes of giving and receiving are conscious and intentional.

Values: Mutual *appreciation; accepting* the other partner as they are; *sharing* symbols of love; making an effort to show the other partner that he or she is *worthy* and *deserving; thankfulness* and, in return, *giving* to show acceptance of shared symbols. The giver is seen as equally worthy and deserving of gratitude, appreciation, and love. Inherent in this value system is the understanding that gifts are unconditional, that is, independent of expectations of giving and/or receiving. This is why romantic gifts are almost always a surprise to the receiver.

Role behavior by illustration:

The giving partner takes Friday afternoon off from work; buys flowers; makes reservations for a moonlight dinner on a riverboat; leaves a note with the flowers at the receiver's place of work informing her to be ready for an evening out; disappears until the appointed time; arrives in a rented luxury car; picks up "date" partner. The two enjoy dinner and dancing on the water, then drive home via their old kissing place on the mountain overlooking the city. (For those on a tighter budget, I'll add that this rather expensive date could have been just as romantic if the giver had arranged a moonlight picnic at their old kissing place.)

DIALOGUE:

Receiver (upon being picked up for their date):

[Passionate kisses given and received]

"Wow! What a surprise to receive all those flowers and your romantic note. The other people at work wish they had a partner as wonderful as you. So where are we going, or is that a surprise, too?"

[More kisses and hugs]

Giver: "It's still a surprise, with lots more in store."

Throughout the evening, the receiver beams at the giver, makes occasional comments about how wonderful the giver is to take such time and effort to show his affection. Remarks are given and received as a way of appreciatively reviewing their relationship—the good times, the special times, the uniqueness of their relationship.

Receiver (several days later): "I still can't get over how wonderful you are to have made those romantic arrangements for us to be together last Friday night. You make me feel so special; you let me know that you think and feel our relationship is still as special as you did when we were single and dating. (More expressions of the receiver's sincere gratitude follow over the next couple of weeks.)

In this example, we have seen only one side of the romantic giver–receiver relationship. While the giver may have lavished tangible gifts on his or her loved one, the receiver has a far less measurable store of gifts to bestow upon the giver. Looks, words, gestures, and other nonverbal communication at the time of receiving and over subsequent days and weeks create a permanent record in their relationship that the giver is also the receiver.

In order to perpetuate the giving–receiving cycle, do you think the receiver eventually becomes the giver? Certainly. Their role definition requires it!

WHY WE FAIL IN OUR ROLES

Intimate relationship unhappiness can be due to many of the factors we have discussed in this chapter:

- The purpose contained in the paradigm of the relationship has been fulfilled or completed, and the partners are not yet conscious of this closure.
- The paradigms being lived out by each of the partners are in conflict.
- The roles of the partners are unclear or conflicting.
- The partners are operating on different sets of values, or their values are unclear.
- The partners are not skilled enough or properly trained to play out their roles in the relationship.
- The partners are operating on different sets of expectations.

Conflicts and unfulfilled potentials in relationships can arise in a way similar to the situation of stage actors who are not thoroughly rehearsed in their roles. If one actor plays out his lines but the other does not respond or responds inappropriately, then there is conflict or loss of continuity in the role play. For the stage play or relationship to be credible and fulfilling for both the actors and the audience, the actors' roles and performances must be congruent and blend smoothly.

As you define and move into new paradigms in your partnership, be patient with yourself and your mate. Look toward each other as your source for feedback on how you are doing and how well your relationship is doing. Compare where you are to where you were a month ago.

Do not compare your progress to other couples, except as models for learning. Encourage each other when times get rough. Celebrate your breakthroughs and successes.

And always keep in mind that you have unseen coaches helping you. They will not intrude into your personal relationship, but when you ask for help they are always delighted to give it. Building, nurturing, and developing your relationship into a functional, sacred partnership is one of the most prized goals your Guardian Angel wishes you to achieve. When you forget your ego and its needs, insights and wisdom will come to you like the lines given by a prompter to actors onstage.

15

When the Sacred Relationship Ends

This chapter explains why and how sacred relationships end. It will help prepare you for this possibility, offer suggestions on how to deal with it, and help you to be aware of the signs that a sacred relationship is over. It explains that once you become a competent partner in a sacred relationship, you may be able to experience continued spiritual growth only through another sacred relationship or series of partners. This is true for both partners, so there are no victims and no perpetrators, only beneficiaries and ambassadors of spiritual evolution.

EXCERPT FROM A PERSONAL LETTER TO A FRIEND

My sacred relationship with Alara has come to an end. It is not as though this was unexpected. We never did have a romantic relationship; ours was a spiritual working relationship. I thought the work we had to do was as spiritual teachers. Not so! The work we were to do was to figure out our emotional issues, using our emotional immaturity as a process for spiritual growth. When we had given each other all we could give, and had taken all we could take, then it was finished. A developmental sacred relationship such as we have had is much like good, productive psychotherapy: The therapist leads the patient as far as she can, and the client learns as much from the therapist as he can. When that point has been reached, remaining together would be unproductive, even detrimental, to the healing and developmental growth of the client. Then it is time to end the formal relationship, become friends, and enjoy each other's company.

That is almost exactly the way Alara and I have completed our formal relationship. We now desire to return our relationship status to how it was before we became engaged. We love each other, we are friends, and we enjoy each other's company, but we do not intrude or have expectations and obligations for each other.

So, dear friend, life gives us chapters. Sometimes for books, sometimes just for living and learning.

Am I jaundiced about intimate relationships? Not at all! That is because when we are truly on the developmental spiritual path, a new partner will come into our life as our growth requires—for greater personal, intimate, loving fulfillment—without the need to cast any aspersions upon the last partner. Our growth is not about comparisons but about increments of growth that are emotionally measurable in wonderful ways.

So rejoice with me as this phase passes, and do not be saddened for the author of *Sacred Relationships*. The last chapter I need to write is about the paradigms of relationships and the expectations, values, roles, and behaviors that characterize each of them. Clarity about these issues is needed, and I simply have had to live out the process of clarity myself before I could offer it to anyone else.

Love and hugs,
Your friend,

Daniel Raphael

THE SADNESS OF ENDINGS

I was recently at a conference where a number of people wanted to ask questions about sacred relationships. So, we arranged a quiet meeting by a large fireplace. We had a beautiful view of a pine forest with mountains in the background. It was a good setting for intimate discussions about intimate subjects.

One question that kept coming up in various forms—one that I had difficulty answering so that the answer was heard and understood—was this: "When will I finally get my ultimate, last relationship?" This question also took the form of "When will I meet my perfect partner?" "Do all my relationships have to end?" "How can I live with so much sadness at the ending of meaningful relationships?" "How will I know when the right one comes along?" And many more, all of which pointed to the same situation—our aversion to the sadness we all must face when relationships come to an end.

Of all situations in relation to other people, the most difficult, it seems, is bringing to closure a relationship that has reached its fullness, whatever form and dimension that may take. A relationship between two people is like a one-gallon milk jug—it can only contain 128 ounces. Once it is full, it cannot be filled any further. Also like a milk jug, a relationship can be emptied and filled up again and again. But who wants to go through repeated "crash and burn" relationship situations with your partner where you go as far as you can, have a big blow-up and then reconcile, blow up, reconcile, blow up, and reconcile over and over again?

For me it is better to just face the facts: Recognize the relationship has become all that it can become, bring a peaceful and loving closure to it, and move on. But ultimately, there is something almost sad about that, isn't there? Yet, that is the nature of relationships between people who desire to grow but who simply cannot grow together any longer.

The key to understanding why intimate relationships come to an end is in that last sentence—*grow*. When we grow, we change. The sadness we pray to avoid occurs only when we grow and our partner does not grow with us—or when our partner grows and we do not grow with him or her. The sadness we loathe occurs only when the relationship paradigm does not grow along with the needs of the partners.

It is ironic that only when you and your partner do not grow, and only when your shared relationship does not develop, can you enjoy and maintain the level of satisfaction that you have achieved. In other words, everything about you, your partner, and your relationship remains static: The old status quo is maintained. But is this what you ultimately want— no change and no growth?

Pause a few moments now to consider that last question. If you answered yes, stop and consider the consequences of a relationship that does not change.

It's an odd scenario, is it not? On one hand, you can have some semblance of happiness at the expense of not growing. Yet on the other hand, you must face the real potential of sadness, for if you continue to grow, you might outgrow the relationship and your partner, or your partner might outgrow you.

It is no wonder that the people who were sitting in the small group with me were genuinely perplexed about finding their ultimate partner and sacred relationship. Each of them knew that just as the sun will rise tomorrow, it is almost as certain that their relationships will undergo major changes, and perhaps end too. This made them more sad about the possibility of yet another relationship ending. They realized that if the author of this book, *Sacred Relationships,* could not keep his intimate relationship from ending, that surely their relationships now and in the future would eventually change and possibly come to an end too.

We are thus faced with a daunting emotional horizon: that we will perennially be faced with the ending of meaningful, intimate love relationships, bringing emotional turmoil and sadness. How much of this must we go through in order to find and be in our last, ultimate, perfect sacred relationship?

That question keeps coming up in one form or another: When?

The answer comes in several forms. First, *we must change our beliefs about how relationships operate.* If we understand and believe that relationships evolve, grow, and change, *then we must change our expectations for our intimate relationships.* If we believe our relationships will change, and if we expect that they must, then we can plan our lives in accordance with how we react to those changes. Then the emotional impact of the realization that our most meaningful intimate love relationship is coming to an end will not devastate us and destroy us.

I am here to tell you that you will feel sadness—I won't try to kid you or deceive you in any way about that. Being fully aware of the powerful dynamics of a continually changing intimate relationship did not eliminate the powerful sadness and the gut-wrenching emotions I felt when Alara and I had our discussion about ending our relationship. It was there, all right—as it should have been.

If we come to the end of an intimate relationship and we do not feel that wrenching emotional twist in our belly, then we have stayed far too long in it. That's a sure sign that the relationship really ended weeks, months, perhaps even years ago. When we feel no emotional pain, that's evidence that we have had little emotional investment in it for a long time; it's likely evidence we have wasted our time in a hollow, unfulfilling relationship.

On the other hand, sadness at the ending of an intimate relationship is evidence that we are still growing, that we are not emotionally dead. It is evidence that we are still on the evolutionary spiral of emotional and spiritual growth. It is evidence that we have not yet found our ultimate, perfect, and stabilized sacred relationship and partner. It means that we still have more growing to do, more emotional challenges to face, and more spiritual understanding and wisdom to gather to our soul.

THE JOY OF NEW BEGINNINGS

Ah, friends, there is also joy in the conscious ending of a meaningful, intimate relationship—joy in the recognition of the transformation, the ascendancy, the transcendence of the old relationship in order for the new one to come into being. Joy in the appreciation of the fullness of a relationship that has run its course, reached its fulfillment. That is an accomplishment to relish!

All that is needed to feel this joy in the passing of a relationship that has fulfilled its chosen paradigm is a change of attitude, of beliefs, and—most necessary—a change of expectations. If indeed relationships are subject to change, then our conscious and intentional guidance of those changes will yield a time of harvest, *the fulfillment of expectations, where fruition is achieved.* When there is a genuine completion, there is opportunity for new beginnings, new challenges, new growth—and the opportunity to engage in our next phase of emotional and spiritual growth.

Asking these questions can open us up to receive our next right and perfect partner: Who will that next partner be? Where is she or he? What new challenges will that person present to me? What insights, what soul wisdom will I be able to share with my new partner for her growth?

FINDING OUR NEXT PARTNER

I can recall that when I was in college, finding my right and perfect next girlfriend was as easy as looking out across the campus when classes were changing. She was always easy to spot. She had the right color hair, right style clothes, and that certain way she walked. Yep, I could spot her a mile away.

Now that I am older and on the spiritual path, discovering my right and perfect next partner is not quite as easy. Now when I look out across a crowd of people in a restaurant, theater, supermarket, or at a conference, I am not so sure that my first pick is the best pick. In fact, I am usually very critical of my first choices. Over the years of working with angels, I have come to rely upon a far better way of finding my right and perfect next partner. I call this approach to finding that person *the Zen of meeting my right and perfect next partner.* That is, by not looking, I find her!

It works this way: (1) I make my intention known to the universe (God, the angels, *et al.*) that I wish to be brought to my right and perfect next partner, or that she be brought to me; (2) I look without expectation of finding her. By looking without expectation I am led to her (the last thing I want to do is to *make* this meeting happen); (3) I jump into the "pool" to meet as many candidates as I possibly can.

Step 3 does involve some conscious thought on my part. As we saw in chapter 13, I set some boundaries, and make specific requests, to help my Guardian Angel bring me into contact with "her." I go to places where likely candidates might be. I am not looking for just any partner; I am expecting that my right and perfect next partner will appear in my life. What I have learned is how to let my Guardian Angel and "her" Guardian Angel arrange the meeting. A celestial helper named Ahsha was instrumental in arranging the circumstances for Alara and me to meet. Angels love a good coincidence, one that is spontaneous, is unanticipated, and is right on.

Step 3 can be boiled down to this simple tactic: No contacts, no new partner—even with angelic help. So get out there and mix with all kinds of people. Enjoy yourself. Enjoy meeting potential partners but without any expectation that the next one is the "right one." When I started doing that, I really began to enjoy myself enjoying other people. Then others began to take notice of me as a good social mixer and social participant. That's when some of those candidates began to look me in the eye so that I felt as if they were reading the inscriptions in my soul. And of course I was doing the same thing too.

Life is a series of passing phases, which includes our intimate and personal relationships. If you think they end, then they do. If you think they just change form, they do that, too, which is the more accurate way of interpreting our relationships. My relationship with Alara hasn't ended;

it just changed form. The immense love that we shared, the doubled-over laugh-til-I-cried moments, will never go away. They will always exist. "Real love lasts." It really does. The real love that we enjoyed in our intimate married relationship still exists. It will never go away. Our partnership was not a hollow, meaningless experience just because the formal marriage ended. I appreciate that tremendously. Those moments are mine and will never be lost just because I intentionally chose to participate in bringing our marriage to a close. Those moments mark the growth of my capacity to love another person, and myself. I know that my capacity to love has increased because I enter the future without any bitter feelings, animosity, anger, or disappointment, but only love and appreciation for what we experienced. I *grew*. So did Alara.

That relationship is a part of the continuum of growth that I will experience for the rest of my life. Just because one relationship ends does not mean that we are not capable of being in an intimate relationship. It only means that the one that is ending, is ending. That's all. We will always be in relationship to someone, particularly with ourselves. By being in intimate relationship with another person, we learn how to be in intimate relationship with ourselves. By striving to be in sacred relationship with another person, we are taking a powerful and meaningful step to be in sacred relationship with ourselves. When we are in an ongoing, functioning sacred relationship with another person, and it goes on and on and on without interruption, then that is a healthy reminder that we, as individuals, are in pretty good shape as a sacred relationship partner to ourselves. When we finally become a whole and complete sacred relationship partner with ourselves, then we will most likely be well prepared to be in an ongoing, perpetuating sacred relationship with our ultimate right and perfect partner.

QUESTIONS AND ANSWERS

The following questions came up during our discussion group. The answers are an amplification of some of the points covered in this lesson.

What makes some sacred relationships end?

There are three reasons why a sacred relationship may come to an end before physical death:

Both partners have progressed as far as they can in that relationship. This is the most positive reason why a sacred relationship comes to an end. When two people in a sacred partnership look back and see where they were as individuals when they came together, and find that they have grown so much that they have nothing left to give to each other, then it may be time to part ways. What the couple should not do in this situation is to remain in the relationship if it means they become static or regress in their spiritual and emotional development.

One partner has outgrown the other. In our society, it is not unusual for one partner to outgrow the other. This is evident when a partner has been striving to aid the other to grow in one or several areas without any positive results. This phase may last months, sometimes even years. This situation is a difficult one to bring to closure because the advanced partner may feel guilty for bringing the relationship to a close and the other partner may feel resentment.

The advanced partner will know when to bring the relationship to a close when she begins to feel that she can no longer remain in the relationship without regressing to her partner's stage of growth.

One partner is holding both back from growing. In this case, one of the partners is unable to resolve old, destructive emotional patterns he brought into the relationship. This may become apparent through the courtship and engagement periods, or it may surface days, months, or years after the partners have made a permanent commitment to each other. In other words, the partner is "stuck" emotionally and is unable to resolve his or her old patterns.

In this situation, the responsible party recognizes this and brings this to the attention of the partner. This then becomes the basis of the couple's shared decision to end the relationship. It is possible that a partner has determined that he is satisfied with where he is in life emotionally and spiritually and does not want to continue the struggle or has determined that he is unable to progress. It is legitimate for a partner to want to quit: Sacred relationships are a lot of work, and it may be better to work on difficult personal issues without the added strains of partnership.

I agree with those statements, but isn't it a judgment call by one or both the partners when to end the relationship? And what about the commitment they made to the relationship and to each other?

Yes to the first question, and, yes, the commitment is definitely involved in the initial decision to be together.

In a sacred relationship, the commitment is to several things: First, there is commitment to the relationship; second, to each other; and third, the commitment that each has to themselves, individually. Look at the word "commitment" as meaning the same as "responsibility." In the first case, as a partner I have a responsibility to assist my partner to grow emotionally and spiritually. In the second case, as a partner I have a responsibility to help the relationship grow emotionally and spiritually. And in the third case, I have a responsibility to my own emotional and spiritual growth. So, yes, it is a definite matter of a judgment call. This will be cleared up as some of the following questions get answered.

Are sacred relationship partners limited just to their own personal resources to resolve conflicts and/or to grow emotionally or spiritually?

No, definitely not. Making the determination to end a sacred relationship is a great deal easier when a couple has used all the resources they can to resolve the block in their relationship. This, too, is a judgment call. For couples who have the means to use all the outside assistance available, the decision will be a great deal clearer and easier to make.

If destructive patterns cannot be resolved within the relationship, then traditional and/or alternative therapies and healing techniques should be used to break these patterns. Failure to break old, destructive emotional and behavior patterns will hold a person back from emotional and spiritual progress, and may also hold the partner back. These patterns can take dozens of forms, from spontaneous disempowerment (acting out the powerless-spouse role) to rage attacks used to avoid examination of behavior and motives.

Daniel, you mentioned some rather strong emotional situations occurring within the context of a sacred relationship (shouting, red faces, waving arms, rising volume of speech, and so on). Aren't sacred relationships above such behavior?

No. The sacred relationship is not an idealistic, peaceful, placid, or totally safe place emotionally. A sacred relationship is an open platform where we can be authentically ourselves, even if that means sometimes shouting and getting red in the face. In the sacred relationship, when this occurs, the best response is for one or both partners to recognize that the emotional activities are *symptoms* of unresolved emotional issues. This is more effective than focusing on the emotions and emotional behavior themselves, which can divert attention into trying to resolve the episode without looking into the deeper reasons for the outburst.

When both partners get sucked into an emotional episode, it is a good deal harder to make the observation that it was/is simply symptomatic of unresolved emotional or ego issues. This recognition often occurs after the heat of the emotional episode has cooled off and the partners begin to sort out the pieces of what happened and why. Then such incidents can be used as a learning tool for growth and increased bonding. That is the heart of the best of sacred relationship interaction.

16

Qualities, Values, and Skills of Functional and Sacred Relationships

The foundation of functional and sacred relationships is the set of qualities and values the partners choose for their partnership, plus the skills to fulfill them. A successful relationship requires the joint decision and commitment of each partner to begin, plus the will, courage, and perseverance to continue.

Learning to be in a sacred relationship is like becoming an accomplished athlete or musician. For every hour spent in front of an audience, hundreds of hours must be spent rehearsing and preparing. Likewise, before meeting our right and perfect partner, we must spend a great deal of time and energy in preparation. Fortunately, we can practice our partnering skills in our other relationships!

Relationship partners and accomplished athletes or musicians both have to continually keep practicing if they are to proficiently perform the hundreds of individual components involved in a single skill. Think of the relatively simple sport of throwing a javelin. As the athlete prepares to throw the javelin, what does he or she do first? Without the javelin in hand, he warms up his muscles, stretches his ligaments, and works his joints. Next, with javelin in hand, eyes focused on a spot on the ground past the limit of his last throw, he prepares his mind, building the emotional, psychic, and spiritual energy to carry and then throw the javelin to that point or farther. Hundreds of hours are spent practicing before the shaft is thrown to its destination.

Functional and sacred relationship partners must practice with just as much diligence, care, and thoughtfulness for the times when they are together.

THE DECISION

The decision to begin a sacred relationship can be made at any time; however, we must be fully conscious of what we are entering into. Consciousness of the depth of our commitment requires that both partners fully discuss the implications of the decision. That's because there are two sides to the experience of being in a sacred relationship: The first is that we get to experience and develop the full social, emotional, and spiritual potential that exists in the fullness of our own being. The second is that we will experience emotional pain as we look into and remove the emotional baggage we brought into the relationship. Fortunately, our emotional issues are finite and quantifiable, whereas the social, emotional, and spiritual potential that exists within each of us is *infinite!* Being in a sacred relationship is the domain of infinite possibilities for two people. Maintaining a state of continual awareness (consciousness) of being in a sacred relationship, with its inherent responsibilities, will be a perpetual function of the partnership.

The decision and declaration of intent to be in a sacred relationship is like drawing a line in the sand that demarcates a new territory in our life. Okay, you have made your decision. Now what is your intent for being in a sacred relationship? This is not a rhetorical question but one that requires each partner to sit down and *write out* their intent for being in a functional or sacred relationship.

TABLE OF RELATIONSHIP QUALITIES, VALUES, AND SKILLS

The table on page 172 represents a minimal operational definition of functional and sacred relationships. Just as a cake recipe is an operational definition of an actual cake, this table is a recipe for functional and sacred relationships. *Perform* the skills required and you will end up with a functional and/or sacred relationship.

The ideal qualities are listed in the left column. In the center column are the values that support the qualities. Each value is fulfilled by hundreds of skills, abilities, behaviors, and practices, some of which are listed in the right column. The movement is from the stated ideals to our daily behaviors—what we do.

For qualities ask "What enduring qualities do we want in our relationship?" For values ask "What do we value that supports the qualities we want in our relationship?" For skills ask "What am I actually willing to *do* that develops the qualities and values we want in our sacred relationship?" Again, only through practicing the skills of functional and sacred relationships will you be able to create the relationship you want. You will need to wrestle with your behavior, words, thoughts, beliefs, and expectations every day of your shared relationship—on your own and with your partner—to achieve this goal. Sure it's tough, but it can be done. *A relationship is a process to be lived rather than an object or status to be achieved.* If you can do it for this moment, you can do it in the next moment as well. The infinite potential of your sacred relationship is only a moment away.

QUALITIES

Listed in the first column are specific qualities that are directly related to the existence of the functional/sacred relationship. They are related to and supported by the values listed in the values column.

Qualities, Values, and Skills
of Both Functional and Sacred Relationships

Qualities	Values	Skills
Trust	Honesty, truthfulness, respect, loyalty, faithfulness	Devotion, discretion, consistency, openness, self-revelation, availability, living consciously in the moment with our partner
Love	Acceptance, appreciation	Generating in our partner feelings of being *worthy* and *deserving* by living consciously in the moment when we are with them: listening; being attentive, caring, affectionate
Cooperation	Participation, coordination, consulting	Listening, supporting, sharing, consulting, giving/taking, giving/receiving, sharing/receiving, letting go/releasing
Discernment	Discretion, patience, forbearance	Examining, analyzing, comparing, weighing, estimating, judging, valuing, choosing, deciding
Intimacy	Authenticity, vulnerability, genuineness	Listening, accepting, sharing, confiding, being open and available
Boundary Setting	Selfhood, individual identity, exclusivity	Setting limits, barriers, perimeters, and territory; respecting privacy; modesty
Sacredness	Valuing spiritual connectedness with all people, valuing all individuals as self and as children of the Creator	Perceiving our partner as being on their own spiritual journey; relating to them where they are on the spiritual path; valuing them in the moment as having neither less nor more value than ourselves; supporting and assisting our partner to achieve the state of Christ or Master Consciousness

Trust and *love* are central qualities of any enduring intimate and personal relationship. These two qualities are the most difficult to fully establish and develop, but will be the most enduring and the last to erode or be destroyed if the relationship goes on the rocks. As my daughter, Rebecca, said of the shared love she and her brother realized they had after a spat when they were kids, "Real love lasts, even after fights and troubles." Real love will endure, even if it is no longer actively shared.

Perhaps *cooperation* could be eliminated and assumed to be an aspect of love and trust. But I think not. Cooperation provides a willingness to be with, work with, and support the activities of our partner. Perhaps another word would convey a similar value, such as "collaboration" or "participation." But "cooperation" conveys the ideal that two people want to work together, so they consciously interact with each other as an active aid and support in the other's emotional, social, and spiritual journey.

Discernment, intimacy, and *boundaries* are related to the two ethical positions discussed in chapter 10: *connectedness without violating boundaries* (connectedness without emotional enmeshment) and *separateness without isolation* (separateness without co-dependency and control). These three central qualities choreograph the dance of intimacy that is necessary for two people to attain oneness of purpose and being without becoming enmeshed and/or co-dependent. These three qualities become central to the vitality, existence, and maintenance of the sacred relationship and for unlocking the psychospiritual potential of each partner.

In both functional and sacred relationships, the partners become agents for each other's personal growth, helping each other to work through emotional issues and to develop and express the potential that lies within each of them.

A *sacred relationship* is qualitatively different from a functional relationship. It assumes all of the qualities of a functional relationship and *adds the values of infinite relationships*. That is, it assumes that this relationship will be one of thousands of relationships that we will experience after this lifetime is finished. For mortals, sacred relationships are fundamental to our eternal future as spiritual partners with others in the endless quest for God.

For an example of how to use the chart, let's examine more closely one specific quality listed in the chart: trust. To have the *quality* of trust in a relationship, partners must use *skills* for discerning the *values* that support the quality. For example, we must distinguish honesty from dishonesty, loyalty from disloyalty, dedication from desecration, devotion from perversion, truthfulness from deceitfulness, and discretion from indiscretion. It does not take much ability to discern the difference between honesty and dishonesty in a black-and-white type of situation. But to more finely develop our relationship skills, we must be able to discern the shadings of dishonesty. We would begin by looking for any evidence of deceit, which inevitably causes doubt and lack of confidence, and eventually separation.

If we detect elements of untrustworthiness in our partner, we should begin to wonder why he or she uses values of distrust. Rather than opting out of the relationship at the first sign of untrustworthiness, which would mean dismissing any undeveloped potential that may remain in the relationship, we should withhold judgment that the other person is dishonest, deceitful, or socially perverted in some way. Rather, we should begin by asking a very elementary question: "Why does my partner use values of distrust in our relationship?" After you ask yourself that question and try to answer it, ask your partner the same question.

Do you see what is happening in this example? Questioning leads us on and on, farther and farther into the labyrinth of a person's psyche and eventually into the origins and development of that psyche. People who use relationship values and skills that keep them in separation from others do so for many, many reasons.

VALUES

The values listed in the middle column are nearly synonymous with their respective quality. They support that quality, and in fact embody it. The values enlighten and give fuller depth of meaning and definition to the quality; this fuller definition helps us more creatively incorporate the ideal quality into our relationship skills.

Just as qualities have transcendent permanence, so do the values that support them. The values of functional and sacred relationships are not transitory, nor are they culturally based; they are not a function of social obligation or social mores. If a value is in vogue as being merely fashionable or bound to a certain time or place, then it does not belong in the table.

For example, being stolid—impassive—was valued in the character of men in prior eras. But in our contemporary culture, people who insist that being stolid is important now seem like dinosaurs. The conditions that called for stolidity no longer exist; except under unusual circumstances, our physical survival is not daily in jeopardy. Today, being stolid is detrimental to connectedness with others and being whole in ourselves.

During the current transition period from the Masculine Era to the Feminine Era, survival values are less needed and can even cause separation from others. What is of value now for the survival of self, family, and community is less individualistic willfulness and more willingness to seek wholeness and unity.

This era marks the transition from the masculine value of "I" to the feminine value of "we." "I" is exclusive, while "us" and "we" are inclusive. "I" is self in separation, while "we" is self in union with others. "We" are on this planet together. Example: If my neighbors in foreign countries suffer because of the pollution "I" have put into the air, then "we" all suffer. The feminine value systems do not see self apart from others but self as a part of the whole. This is the new frontier, men!

Taking the example of the word "stolid" a bit further, the synonyms for "stolid" include "detached," "dispassionate," "impassive," "imperturbable," "unimpassioned," and "unruffled." It is interesting that the opposites of those words include "attached," "passionate," "emotional," "perturbable," "impassioned," and "capable of being ruffled." To have a relationship that is functional and healthy, we need to develop a balanced, positive expression of all these qualities. In other words, I have to participate in the relationship without being either emotionally enmeshed or emotionally disconnected. Do you think that takes a lot of practice and training? You bet it does! A male in these transition years must have proficiency in *discernment* to avoid offending women by being either aloof or solicitous.

SKILLS

Using skills of functional and sacred relationships is where the tire meets the road, when theory takes a back seat to application. We are challenged, moment to moment, to consciously and intentionally use functional relationship skills to make tough decisions for high stakes and long-term results.

Incorporating relationship skills in everyday life means using knowledge, training, practice, confidence, and the opportunity for spontaneous expression of values to produce functional relationship qualities.

A conscious and intentional sacred relationship with our partner is one of the safest places to receive reflections and insights about our emotional issues. In this powerful relationship—after we come home from work or a similar situation where our buttons have been pushed—we have a sacred space where we can explore with our partner our feelings of anger, resentment, and frustration. We can explore the roots of our dysfunctional relationship practices, beliefs, and expectations while learning and practicing new relationship skills.

To use an extended metaphor, functional, empowering relationship skills are much like professional carpentry skills: They require intentional application of our will and an investment of time, energy, and the patience to "bend a few nails" in order to become more fully skilled at building the rooms and houses we will live in for the rest of our mortal and infinite lives.

The "house of our life" is built with the "boards of our decisions" to create the "rooms of our relationships" using the "hammers, squares, saws, and nails" from our toolchest of skills. What kind of house do you live in? Was it built with a design in mind? Or is it a surrealistic contortion of misshapen rooms? Is it an expression that provides for joy and fulfillment for you?

Many of us were not trained in the skills necessary to construct comfortable relationships. For many of us, the "on-the-job training" we received early in life allowed us to get by. But as adults, are our relationships a barrio of shacks or a subdivision of high-end designed houses, or a combination of the two?

DISCERNING QUALITIES, VALUES, AND SKILLS

It is as instructive to know what we don't want in our relationships as to know what we do want. This is where the critical skill of discernment is necessary. The root meaning of the word "discern" tells us that weighing, estimating, and comparing are important functions in applying the skills of functional relationships.

Let's say we wanted to discern, for example, whether a relationship is abusive and should not be continued. If we are unable to question the pain we experience in relationships, if we are unable to decide we do not want painful relationships in our life, if we are unable to will and take action to end that terror, then abuse will continue in our minds and in our relationships until we die. However, when we do begin to question the worth of our painful relationships and decide to end them, and *will* to discern and practice the skills and values of functional relationships, only then can we move forward to joy, fulfillment, emotional stability, and spiritual enlightenment.

Here's another example of the importance of discernment: New partners who are aware of the dysfunctional relationship values, skills, beliefs, and interpretations of their partner's family will often try to help their partner overcome them. Two of the most difficult problems new partners will encounter in the process are *enmeshment* and *separation.* Discernment in using the skills of functional relationships is necessary to avoid these extremes. Individuals with dysfunctional relationship training often are unable to discern how far to intrude or how aloof they should be from their partner's emotional dramas.

One extreme is too much *separation* (isolation, disconnection, feeling cut off) from others. Those in separation (loners and recluses) are saying in effect that they do not need people in their lives, that they are everything they need to be complete. This is probably an indication that their self-image and self-esteem are so low that they feel unworthy and incapable of helping their partner. This causes distance and isolation between them and their partner, and others as well.

Self-isolation is highly unproductive because we are not fully human outside of a social group. When we are too much alone, we cannot experience and unleash the great social potential that lies within each of us. Alone, we cannot come to know all of the superconscious values of being in relationship with others. How would we learn loyalty, faithfulness, love, caring, compassion, generosity, forgiveness, and love without being in relationships? We simply cannot. We must be in a relationship to explore and express the Master potential that lies within us.

On the other extreme, too much integration with others causes emotional and social *enmeshment,* meaning entanglement or ensnarement. In the extreme, those in enmeshment (co-dependency) are saying in effect that they are nothing without other people and must be emotionally enmeshed to be complete. This causes a loss of self-identity, personhood, and self-esteem. When a couple is enmeshed, the problems of one seem to be the problems of the other, and each is trying to solve the other's problems, believing erroneously that they are the same.

Enmeshment and separation are like jackals and hyenas that require our wary attention to avoid becoming entrapped by them. Continued involvement in either may cause the relationship to be devoured by one of these extremes.

It takes persistent, proficient, and discerning use of relationship skills—applying the values of functional relationships—to consistently produce the qualities of the relationship we desire. It also takes persistent and conscious effort not to act out the erroneous beliefs and expectations we learned in our formative years. It is very helpful to have a friend or a support group help us develop those skills. This can relieve one or both partners of some of the shared responsibilities, which is particularly useful during the vulnerable time when a relationship is still young.

SELF-CARING IS A SKILL

Self-caring is the middle ground between being too intrusive and too remote from our partner. Self-caring also means self-nurturing, and serves to support us so that we can participate effectively in a shared relationship without being too detached from our partner or too self-absorbed.

A broad goal of being self-caring is to nurture and care for ourselves so that we can become the best person possible. Then we can avoid stagnation, the bane of relationships that aren't growing. We will become more interesting to be with, more well-rounded as individuals, and hopefully equals to our partners, who are also nurturing their own potential.

In order to maintain a functional relationship, we must care enough about ourselves as a fifty-percent participant in the relationship that we neither give our half away to our partner by becoming enmeshed nor leave our fifty percent of the relationship idle by being aloof.

Self-caring also means being responsible for ourselves. This is different from being *selfish,* which is caring for ourselves at the expense of others, or from being *co-dependent,* which is caring for others at the expense of ourselves.

Being self-caring, I remain me, and you remain you. The combination of you and me in relationship creates us—not another, separate entity but the *process* of you and me.

Us is not *me. Us* is not *you.*

You is not *us. You* is not *me.*

Me is not *us. Me* is not *you.*

We is *us,* and *us* is *we.*

The point of this Dr. Seuss–like grammatical wreckage is: A relationship is a process separate from the individual identities of the partners. It is not another entity like a corporation. To enter into a relationship with another person is to co-create a distinct process. It is like the joint ownership of an automobile a couple has bought. Both own it and both use it. The partnership is a process of many different functions that coordinate to provide a consistent and reliable form of transportation. The car is best maintained when the individuals have accepted a schedule of maintenance and service for it, vacuum and wash it, and wax and polish it as it ages.

A relationship is a similar process involving many different functions: It must be maintained by the owner-drivers, and the owner-drivers must participate in its operation to get to where they want to go in it. To extend this metaphor a bit further, examine the driving skills you use when you are in your cars (relationships). Do you drive them hard and then trade them in for another when their usefulness is gone? Or do you diligently take care of your cars and drive them within their capabilities?

If you do take care of your cars (relationships), where did you learn those skills? Probably from other drivers you watched as you grew up. Or you learned them on your own because it became too expensive and too painful to be stranded on the road of life out in the middle of nowhere, with no other cars coming along. The quality of the operation of your cars and relationships reflects the skills and values that you practice in relation to them.

◆

Anything of value takes time to bring into being, as the cliché goes. If this is true, then a lifetime of effort will be required to help us develop relationships that are infinitely durable for our eternal spiritual journey, beginning right here on this material planet. Right now, we are learning the relationship skills that will directly aid our spiritual evolution. To evolve spiritually, we must practice those skills with increasing proficiency. Our functional/sacred relationship partner is our greatest ally to help us evolve and develop all of our personal, social, and spiritual potential.

Afterword

An Educational Continuum
for Functional and Sacred
Relationships

This manual would not be complete without a discussion of children in the lives of functional and sacred relationship partners. As we have stated many times throughout these lessons, our commitment to be in sacred relationship is first with ourselves. The integrity of that commitment, however, directly extends to our intention to nurture a conscious and intentional sacred relationship with our children, whether they are in our home or with a former spouse. That commitment includes the responsibility to consciously teach our children sacred relationship skills, values, and qualities.

As a final word, let's briefly examine the need for relationship-skill training in our children's lives, and suggest ways that this can be incorporated as part of a continuum of educational development in our homes and in our schools.

THE FOUR "R"s OF BASIC EDUCATION

Reading, 'Riting, 'Rithmetic, and Relationships

Historically, a "good education" was the stairway to personal and social achievement and economic improvement. To be educated has always been a cultural and societal achievement that is highly revered and coveted, especially by those from less fortunate social and economic backgrounds. It is a mark of intelligence, culture, status, and achievement.

Power, influence, earned wealth, social status, and religious position in the twentieth century have always been associated with literate people. Today, no one in any civilized field of endeavor is illiterate! Yet it is ironic that in literate "civilized" nations, effective relationship skills are still acquired in the same manner by which all self-made individuals have always taught themselves—on the streets and on the playing field of hard knocks. How can a society be considered civilized when relationship skills, the foundation of the social and cultural edifice of civilization, are not even considered as basic to a person's fundamental education as the 3 Rs?

Though relationship skills are more fundamental to success in our society than the 3 Rs (reading, writing, and arithmetic), teaching relationship skills is left to parents or parental figures whose own skills in relating all too often tend to be absent, dysfunctional, or marginally functional. Child development psychologists and specialists tell us that the basic personality structures and the kinds of relationships children will try to establish and model for the rest of their lives are determined before age five. Relationship skills are taught by virtually anyone who comes in contact with children during these early developmental stages. But it does not have to be that way.

Effective relationship skills can and should be well developed prior to the first day of school, even before pupils begin learning the 3 Rs. Generally, students who do not possess fundamental functional relationship skills do not do well either academically or socially, even though they may have superior intelligence. Teachers already recognize this factor by lumping these children into a group who "lack adequate social skills."

Remedial relationship skills classes for adults are also needed, to help parents raise their children to become socially functional adults. The well-being of our society is dependent upon parents who model socially functional relationship skills.

A STRATEGY FOR INTENTIONAL RELATIONSHIP TRAINING

This strategy involves teaching children relationship skills appropriate to their developmental capabilities, beginning before birth and continuing until they are able to practice relationship skills on their own, consciously and intentionally.

Relationship skills are just that, skills. They are learned much as we learn to drive a car, write a letter, ride a bicycle, swim, walk, and speak, for example. Think of this challenge as being similar to teaching children how to tie their shoes. The task is broken down into individual steps using teacher demonstration, step-by-step experiential exercises, repeated practice, student demonstration, and actual situations for use. Note that when we teach the skills of functional relationships, the qualities and values of functional relationships are intrinsically included.

A DEVELOPMENTAL CONTINUUM OF RELATIONSHIP SKILL TRAINING

The Procreative Couple

The primary purpose of providing training to parents-to-be is to prepare them to become fully conscious that they are responsible for being the main resource of relationship training for their future children. In other words, they must prepare their children to become functional participants in their own family, community, and the larger society. The secondary purpose is to provide future parents with functional relationship skills for their own relationship.

Prenatal (Conception to Birth)

During this era the parents-to-be provide a positive emotional environment for their baby as though the child were already born. It has been shown that the prenatal social, emotional, and sensory environments of the pregnant mother have a tremendous influence upon the emotional well-being of the child.

Natal and Postnatal (0–3 Months)

Although the new infant seems to be emotionally inert and unresponsive to its surroundings during this period, that is not the case at all; this stage has an immense impact upon the child's emotional and social adjustment for the rest of its life. Basic emotional issues of abandonment, personal value, worthiness, dependence, and independence are given ownership by the child during this time. Primal trust or distrust is developed during this and subsequent eras, and will remain with the child during its adult life. The parents must appreciate this small package as the fully evolved adult it will become.

Subsequent Developmental Eras

From infancy (3–12 months), childhood (1–3 years), and preschool (3–6 years), through the school eras (6–9 and 9–12), preadult (12–15), and adult years (15 and following), the child must be provided with training and education that is appropriate for his or her social relationship skill development. Each developmental era has its own complex of relationship skills that evolve from prior developmental eras. Each skill level contributes to the evolution of the next era.

In adulthood, all relationship skills are brought together. Having completed the continuum of relationship skill development, adults are ready to function as contributing, responsible partners in their society, communities, and families, and ultimately as teacher-trainer-parents of their own children.

WHY TEACH FUNCTIONAL RELATIONSHIP SKILLS?

These skills are fundamental to personal, social, and spiritual happiness. As we have seen in this book, the emotional turmoil and disappointment we feel in relationships is indicative of absent, deficient, or dysfunctional interpersonal relationship skills that relate directly to unresolved intrapersonal mental-emotional issues.

Why teach functional relationship skills? For the same reasons reading, writing, and arithmetic are taught in public schools: to provide the tools and skills necessary to help each individual unlock his or her hidden potential. In practical terms, functional relationship skills are directly related to employee productivity, job satisfaction, customer satisfaction, and personal achievement. On the other hand, when relationship skills are absent or not well developed, unhappiness, relationship anguish, pain, frustration, and other types of emotional distress often result.

Communities and the whole of our society have already made a direct correlation between educational levels and the reduction of divorce, crime, antisocial behavior, delinquency, school dropout rates, and alcohol and drug abuse, for example. Now it is time for communities to understand the positive connection between functional relationship skills and reducing the social costs of these issues.

Wherever individuals with functional relationship skills live, work, and play, all aspects of social interaction are improved. As more functional relationships come into existence, the world we live in becomes more healthy and peaceful. But to accomplish this, we must provide the tools that enable individuals to grow and actualize their potential in the vastness of the social universe.

Give the Gift of Sacred Relationships to Your Friends and Loved Ones

ORDER FORM

❑ Yes, I want _____ copies of *Sacred Relationships* at $15.95 each plus $3.50 shipping for the first book and $1.00 for each additional book.

Name_____

Company _____

Address _____

City _____ State_____ Zip_____

Phone _____

❑   Check or money order enclosed

Please charge my   ❑ Visa   ❑ MasterCard

Card #_____ Exp. _____

Signature _____

Call our TOLL FREE order line: 1-888-267-4446
Or fax your order to: 415-898-1434

Please make your check payable and return to
Origin Press
1122 Grant Avenue, Suite C
Novato, California 94945